AN AUSTRALIAN PERSPECTIVE

And who shall say on what errand the insolent emu

Walks between morning and night on the edge of the plain?

—*James McAuley*
"Terra Australis"

AN
AUSTRALIAN
PERSPECTIVE

R. M. CRAWFORD

The University of Wisconsin Press

Madison, 1960

DU 107
C7

Published by The University of Wisconsin Press
430 Sterling Court, Madison 6, Wisconsin
Copyright © 1960 by the Regents of the University of
Wisconsin

Printed in the United States of America by
Vail-Ballou Press, Inc., Binghamton, New York
Library of Congress Catalog Number 60–11442

TO DOROTHY AND PAUL

Preface

These reflections on Australian history were given as the Knaplund Lectures at the University of Wisconsin in December,
1958, and stand with only minor corrections of phrase and
fact. My first acknowledgment must be to the University of
Wisconsin which, by inviting me for a semester as British Commonwealth Visiting Lecturer, gave me this opportunity to look
at my own country from outside. To such sense of perspective
as distance could supply, something was added by the fact
that these lectures were a return to Australian history after
years spent in other fields. If they are an essay in perspective,
they are also a declaration of faith. Would I have displayed
such confidence nearer to the normal irritations of day-to-day
at home, or, if more recently involved in specialist inquiry,
have dared to declare a faith at all? I do not know the answers
to these questions; but having read these lectures again at
home, I find I stick to them.

They owe much to many people. Two debts I must particularly acknowledge. The name of Paul Knaplund is an
honourable one in historical scholarship, and to deliver the
Knaplund Lectures is to share in some reflection of his distinction. No student of the history of the Second British Empire can neglect his work, and no book is written on this subject which fails to bear witness to his contribution. England
has provided its own historians of its imperial history, and the
best of them have been more than worthy of their wage; but
for encyclopaedic knowledge used with quiet probity and wise
humanity to illuminate rather than to dazzle, it is to a Nor-

wegian American that the history of the British Empire and of the Commonwealth owes one of its greatest debts.

The concluding pages of the first lecture draw heavily on a study of the pastoral society of Victoria written by the late Miss Margaret Kiddle. Miss Kiddle was for many years my research assistant and dedicated her book, *Men of Yesterday,* now in process of publication, to me. Faced with the certainty of untimely death, she worked on at this book until she had finished it, although often the strength even to hold her papers had deserted her. One of her last requests was that I should use what she called my book for my lectures in Wisconsin, and I have done so freely.

I wish also to acknowledge the kind permission of the Melbourne University Press to quote from James McAuley's *Under Aldebaran;* of the Lothian Publishing Company, Melbourne, to quote from *The Poems of Furnley Maurice* (Frank Wilmot); and of the Meanjin Press, Melbourne, to quote from Miss Judith Wright's *The Moving Image.*

R . M . C .

Melbourne, Australia
December, 1959

Contents

AN AUSTRALIAN PERSPECTIVE

I

A *Pastoral Aristocracy*

Australia has presented a commonplace front to the world. Its history has lacked the conventional elements of romance which serve to lend an immediate interest to the history of other new-settled countries. It has fought no war of independence, nor any civil war. Nor were our first settlers opposed by warlike tribes of indigenous inhabitants. Some, applying measures equally superficial, have even found the country itself dull, a country of brilliant light and subtle colourings. But, most of all, I believe, the impression of the commonplace has been built up by the presentation of Australian society as one reduced, by a jealous democratic disapproval of distinction or difference, to the dull mediocrity of an immense suburb,

> Where second-hand Europeans pullulate
> Timidly on the edge of alien shores.[1]

It is my purpose in these three lectures to examine both the stereotype of commonplace Australia and some grounds for finding it misleading. Sometimes, when held by outside observers, it has a superficial source; it is a little difficult, for example, for an educated Englishman to believe that something spoken in a flat Australian accent might be worth pondering. Denis Brogan, one of our more recent visitors, saw through this barrier, but recognized its existence. "And to hear," he wrote in one of your journals, "an intelligent, critical, sardonic conversation (the Australians are admirable talkers)

1. A. D. Hope, "Australia," in George Mackaness, ed., *An Anthology of Australian Verse* (Sydney: Angus and Robertson, 1952).

in an accent which, in England, one associates with near il-
literacy, is a startling experience." [2] But it has been Australians
themselves who have done most to create this impression, and
something more stubborn than a post-war and passing mood
has been expressed by those commentators who have deplored
the suspicious mediocrity of a society in which one of them
finds "intellectual and moral shallowness" and another "a
resentment of distinction." [3]

It is to this last that such laments boil down; to a fear, that
is, that a democratic society abhors distinction and to an
assumption that Australian society has a democratic bias deeply
imprinted on it. It is possible to support this assumption with
impressive evidence, and most Australian historians agree with
the statement of I. D. McNaughtan, a young historian whose
untimely death ended a career of rare promise, that even
without the spur of the gold discoveries, "the Australian
Colonies, with no traditional conservative class and without
established institutions would hardly have left the broad road
from Benthamite liberalism through political democracy towards 'state socialism,' though they might well have travelled
it more slowly." [4]

But this conclusion does not contain the whole truth, and it
conceals some part of the truth by drawing our attention away
from a component in Australian history which is not democratic
but aristocratic. And the further conclusion, which is often
drawn, that Australian democracy has been the cause of cultural mediocrity, drags a red herring across the path of enquiry
into the conditions of cultural maturity. But that is the subject

2. *Harper's Magazine*, June 1958, pp. 62–68.

3. P. H. Partridge, "The Australian Universities," in W. V. Aughterson,
ed., *Taking Stock: Aspects of Mid-Century Life in Australia* (Melbourne:
F. W. Cheshire, 1953); and K. T. Henderson, "Religious Institutions and
Aspirations," in G. Caiger, ed., *The Australian Way of Life* (London:
Heinemann, 1953).

4. Gordon Greenwood, *Australia: A Social and Political History* (Sydney: Angus and Robertson, 1955), p. 99.

of my second lecture; the aristocratic thread in Australian history is the subject of this.

Historians have recognized the existence of aristocratic elements; but they have in general seen them as a foil, an unchanging backdrop, against which to view the real stuff of Australian history, the March of the Demos to its predestined victory. Aristocracy, however, was not a mere backdrop in nineteenth-century Australia, but one of the active partners in a point-counter-point, at times discordant enough, in the course of which a society grew up which was permeated by democratic assumptions, it is true, but which was, nevertheless, through most of the nineteenth century, aristocratic in its structure and in its distribution of authority, to a degree that calls for elucidation.

It is not difficult to understand the dominance of the "dead-level" interpretation of Australian history, for that history began in 1788 with a wretched freight of convicts and ended a cycle with the social welfare programme of Joseph Benedict Chifley and the Australian Labour Party. The successive phases which fill the space between these two poles seem to be merely variations of the theme. In 1831, for example, began the assisted free immigration which swamped the convict population, though still with Britain's "redundant" poor—"the outpourings of the poorhouses," [5] more than one dyspeptic critic complained in those early days. Twenty years later in 1851 began the Australian gold rushes, which reduced all on the fields, whatever their various social origins, to the common level of mole-skins, and allowed only the distinction between the lucky and the unlucky. That same golden decade saw some of the instruments of democratic politics so rapidly gained that by 1859 four of the Australian colonies enjoyed manhood suffrage and four of them the secret ballot. So democratised, the parliaments of the eastern colonies passed laws during the following decade which were designed—in vain, it is sadly admitted—to break

5. Cf. *Cambridge History of the British Empire*, VII, Part I, 265.

the land monopoly of the shepherd kings and to turn the pastoral wilderness into a land of smiling farms, where, in agreement with a dream already long cherished by Australian radicals, they could

> . . . reside
> In a home of [their] own by some clear waterside.[6]

In that heroic phase of Australian historical writing which received its main fillip from the work of Mr. Brian Fitzpatrick in the 1930's, this theme appeared to reach its apotheosis in the militant alliance in the 1880's and 1890's of the trade unions of both town and bush, inspired by utopian ideals in which were blended elements of Henry George, Bellamy, and Australian "mateship," together with some slight spicing from Karl Marx. Defeated in "the great strikes" of the nineties in their attempt to create a New World which should not know the injustices of the Old, they were depicted as licking their wounds, learning new wisdom in the old ways of capitalism, organising the Australian Labour Party and eventually using it to create, albeit imperfectly, the somewhat tempered justice of the social welfare state.

This interpretation inspired and provoked its own revision, much of which has been carried out by students themselves responsive to the radical interpretation of Australian history but whose scholarly training has freed them from its limitations. And part of this revision has been to see, as no mere backdrop for the democratic play, but as a theme in active interplay with it, the attempts that were so often successful, not to create in the Antipodes a new democracy, but to recreate there the classes and the graces of old England.

Our origins offered little help in the way of grace. The "First Fleet" of eleven small ships, which set sail from Plymouth in May, 1787, for Botany Bay in New Holland,

6. From the "The Selector's Song" in W. L. F. Wannan, *The Australian* (Melbourne: Australasian Book Society, 1954), p. 221.

carried convicts, a garrison of marines, and the officers of a gaol. This was no "Mayflower" to which widening circles of descendants would seek to trace their ancestry, but a freight of misery, to be left, if not in silence, at least in the decent anonymity of general description. Nor did the first few years, when a starving settlement struggled merely to survive while wretched convicts scratched the unfamiliar soil with inadequate hoes and still less adequate wills, add much increase of light to those miserable beginnings. The industrious and heroic vision of Captain Arthur Phillip, the first governor; the benign curiosity of Captain Tench of the Marines; the religious humanity of Lieutenant Dawes; the hopeful labours of the ex-convict, James Ruse; these things might shine like tiny candles in the darkness and wickedness of their world; but on balance the future might seem to offer little beyond the efforts of a prison farm to earn enough beyond its needs of subsistence to be able to import those "ardent spirits of Bengal" which inspired its debaucheries and deepened its depravity.

Not many years had passed, however, before signs of a brighter future were evident. Miserable though the circumstances of their birth and upbringing might be, it was widely noticed that the "currency lads and lasses," the native born, were better than their parents. ". . . I only repeat the testimony of persons who have had many opportunities of observing them," wrote Commissioner Bigge, thirty years after the first settlement, "that they neither inherit the vices nor the feelings of their parents." [7]

But it is nearer to my theme to notice that the limited struggle for subsistence was bound, once the hungry years were weathered, to grow into a search for fortune. The expenditure of the British Government on the convict, military, and civil establishments in the colony provided a sustained inflow of capital which gave ample opportunity for commercial specu-

7. Commissioner Bigge, *Report on the State of Agriculture and Trade in the Colony of New South Wales* (1823), p. 81.

lation. The monopolistic activities of the officers of the New South Wales Corps, the Rum Ring, were not without importance in the early history, both moral and economic, of New South Wales; and indeed, if we leave aside the influence of the traffic in rum on an already depraved society, the Rum Ring's monopoly proved a major means of turning the public inflow of capital into the private fortunes of some of the colony's chief entrepreneurs. Captain John Macarthur arrived in Sydney in debt; but as Inspector of Public Works and Paymaster of the New South Wales Corps, the main architect of the officers' monopoly, he was able as early as 1794, to become "one of the most substantial farmers and stock owners in the colony" [8] and the founder of one of its proudest dynasties. As a man of fortune, he could afford to continue those experiments in growing fine merino wool which he was not alone in starting.

Yet the case of Macarthur, "keen as a razor and rapacious as a shark," [9] only wrote in large letters a grasping of opportunity that was general. In an age when to be an Englishman, a Scot, or even an Irishman of education was to be, in Adam Smith's sense of the term, an "improver," the opportunities offered by British official expenditure on the new colony were bound to be improved. With convicts to supply them with labour, and government expenditure to supply the source of capital, the officers of the garrison or of the civil and medical establishments, reinforced on occasion by a free settler such as Robert Campbell, the Calcutta merchant, or by a shrewd emancipated convict such as Simeon Lord, were ready and able to probe the various opportunities for enterprise which might supply them with profit and the colony with a staple product for export.

These experiments were not confined to breeding for fine wool; but for reasons connected with both the English wool

8. *The Australian Encyclopaedia* (Sydney: Angus and Robertson, 1958), V, 403.

9. Cited by Ernest Scott in *Cambridge History of the British Empire*, VII, Part I, 101.

market and the Australian climate, it was evident in 1819, when Commissioner J. T. Bigge was sent by Lord Bathurst to report on the Australian colonies, that fine wool was to be the staple. "Upon the expediency of promoting in the colony of New South Wales the growth of fine wool," he concluded, "and creating a valuable export from thence to Great Britain, no doubt can be entertained . . . as it appears to be the principal, if not the only, source of productive industry within the colony from which the settlers can derive the means of repaying the advances made to them from the mother country, or supplying their own demands for articles of foreign manufacture." [10]

It will be readily understood that selective breeding for fine wool is a big man's business, requiring capital, skill, and broad acres. Despite the early and perfectly natural habit of granting small holdings to ex-convicts and former soldiers of the garrisons, the large pastoral estate quickly came to dominate the Australian rural scene. Demoralisation by rum speeded the frequent failure of the small farmer; but in any case none of the necessary conditions of a sound agriculture yet existed to keep him on his feet—neither a stable market nor adequate transport for a heavy and bulky product; neither knowledge of the peculiar demands of his new country nor grains bred to respond to them. Agriculture lagged far behind the prior occupation of the country by pastoralists, and this was occupation by men of capital and their servants. It took over one hundred years before agriculture could spread extensively into areas previously regarded as designed by Providence for sheep and therefore for the more thinly spread occupation by pastoralists.

Even so, vast areas remained and still remain, too dry for agriculture and apt only for pasture. For Australia away from its coasts is an arid country, in which rainfall declines rapidly both in average amount and in certainty as you move inland. If you would realise this, consider that a journey which would

10. Bigge, *Agriculture and Trade in New South Wales*, p. 18.

take you as the crow flies from Boston to the lush fields of
Madison would take you from Australia's east coast to the
region of what is called Lake Eyre, a lake which held water
in 1851 and again in 1951, but which is usually a vast layer of
salt over mud, almost 3,500 square miles of it lying thirty-nine
feet below sea level. By it stretches the country of the Birdsville
Track, which, wrote C. T. Madigan, geologist and explorer, "is
a fascinating, tantalizing region. In its good seasons, its miles
of waving grasses lure men to their destruction. Once they have
come under the spell of its vast spaces, they cannot leave it.
The grassy plains change to a burning stony desert, the stock
gradually die out, the sand drifts over the pitiful fences and
stockyards, its glaring ridges slowly approach and engulf the
homestead, and yet men hang on. Month after month the
brazen sky is watched; heavy clouds form, to clear away again;
years pass; but some day the cooling torrents will become
swirling yellow maelstroms, and the country will wave with
grass again." [11]

Such country was at the further edge of possibility, even for
thin pastoral occupation and, apart from the tropical North
and the remoter Northwest, it was the last to be occupied; but
the demonstrated promise of Australian fine wool stimulated
an immense wave of pastoral expansion which in the twenty or
thirty years before 1850 carried pastoralists and their sheep
virtually to the ultimate limits of occupation in New South
Wales, Victoria, and South Australia, and lapped the edges
even of that country of the Birdsville Track.

From the time of Bigge's Reports, this expansion was dominated by social ideals which were not at all democratic. John
Macarthur, whose persuasiveness, supported by samples of fine
wool, had gained him a grant of five thousand acres as early as
1805, with a promise of five thousand more, had already estab-

11. C. T. Madigan, *Central Australia* (Oxford University Press, 1936),
p. 140.

lished in Camden the prototype of an Australian gentry. The first stage of harsh acquisition over, his sons and nephews lived the lives of English country gentlemen, pursuing commercial opportunity still as in the Australian Agricultural Company, but also building schools and churches, serving both in local government and on the legislative council of the colony, improving their livestock, leading the Agricultural Society of New South Wales, carrying out botanical research, winning awards of gold medals for this and for experiments in viticulture, establishing in that second generation, the solid tradition of a dynasty. That drive towards the foundation of what William Charles Wentworth described as "respectable establishments" [12] was not confined to the Macarthurs. It was shared by former army officers, such as Edward Charles Close (1790–1866) whose "Closebourne House," set in a large estate in the Hunter River Valley, was "famous for its hospitality"; by officers of the colonial medical establishment such as Close's neighbour, James Bowman, who married John Macarthur's daughter, Mary, and applied for a crown grant of land "commensurate with the stock he had acquired with his wife"; by merchants turned gentleman landowners, such as Thomas Icely (1797–1874) who on his estate of thirteen thousand acres called "Coombing," improved his sheep until they were among the best merinos in the country, bred a valuable herd of Durhams and Herefords, and maintained a stud of thoroughbred horses, breeding police horses, cavalry remounts, and race horses, these last including Sir Hercules, progenitor of Yattendon, Cossack, Zoë, and the Barb, the last of which won the Melbourne Cup in 1866 and all four of which are famous in Australian racing history, which some Australians at least consider the only history worth knowing.[13]

12. A. C. V. Melbourne, *William Charles Wentworth* (Oxford University Press, 1934), p. 23.
13. For the Macarthurs, Close, Bowman, and Icely, see *The Australian Encyclopaedia* (1958), Vols. II and V.

It is not surprising, then, that even in 1821 John Macarthur was advising Commissioner Bigge in favour of aristocratic establishments. Macarthur offered Bigge a means of reconciling those penal purposes and commercial opportunities of the colony which had seemed to be in conflict. Let land be no longer granted in small lots to emancipated convicts and other settlers who lacked capital and who could not improve their holdings; but only in large holdings to "really respectable settlers—men of real capital." These "Proprietors would be desirous to take as many convicts as possible." To Macarthur's calculations, the persuasion was often added that convicts assigned to the service of these respectable settlers in the country would at once be removed from the temptations of the town and exposed to the gentle and improving influences of nature. This latter argument, so much favoured by landowners who were short of labour, was little supported by the experience that shepherds sought forgetfulness of the terrors and the tedium of the bush in alcoholic sprees which ended only when the pay cheque had been drunk through. The rural moralising was a frill, however, and the forecast of aristocratic establishments was genuine enough. The respectable settlers, said Macarthur, "should have estates of at least 10,000 acres, with reserves contiguous of equal extent— Such a body of proprietors would in a few years become wealthy and with the support of Government powerful as an Aristocracy— The democratic multitude would look upon their large possessions with envy and upon the Proprietors with hatred—" but this "democratic feeling" could not be "too soon opposed with vigour." [14]

To this advice Bigge listened, and his recommendations, if differently worded, were in accordance with its tenour. He recommended the extension of the assignment system by which property in the services of convicts for the period of their

14. M. Clark, *Sources of Australian History* (Oxford University Press, 1957), pp. 135–40.

servitude was assigned to private settlers, and discouraged the granting of crown lands to emancipated convicts and to other settlers who lacked the capital and the skill to improve their holdings.

The tide was flowing strongly in favour of the wool growers of New South Wales. Since October, 1819, with other British colonists, they had enjoyed a tariff preference for their wool in the English market. For twenty years until transportation to New South Wales ceased in 1840, their needs of labour were met by a great extension of the assignment system. And land policy, modified in accordance with Bigge's advice in favour of men of capital, was defined more clearly in their favour by the Bathurst Regulations of 1825. These regulations continued the practice of making grants of land, but only to men of capital, the method adopted being to allow 600 acres for every £500 of capital. The Bathurst Regulations also defined methods for the sale of crown lands, providing for auction in lots of 1,920 acres, or three square miles. The limit for any one person was set at five lots, i.e. 9,600 acres, close enough to the area of 10,000 acres which Macarthur had stated to be desirable.

In his *Letter from Sydney* of 1829, written not in Sydney but in Newgate Gaol where Sydney was naturally a commonplace of conversation, Edward Gibbon Wakefield, the "systematic coloniser," so justly described by Professor Knaplund as "this restless schemer," [15] claimed that property was valueless in the colony because labourers could not be found to work it. And they could not be found, he continued, because land was so freely granted that they could easily become themselves landowners. This was quite untrue. For almost a decade when he wrote, land had not been granted to small men without capital, nor had it been easy for labourers to become land-

---

15. *James Stephen and the British Colonial System, 1813–1847* (Madison: University of Wisconsin Press, 1953), p. 76. A just estimate of Wakefield's ability and character is given on pages 93–94 of this work.

owners. Nevertheless, Wakefield's influence, although over-estimated, did confirm a trend in British colonial policy to-wards restricting access to the crown lands to those with the knowledge and capital to develop them. It must be said, how-ever, that official policy was less governed by an exclusive social ideal than by the belief that small grants were useless, a belief confirmed by Bigge's reports of the dilapidation of small hold-ings in New South Wales and Van Diemen's Land and of the drunkenness and indebtedness of their possessors. It is a para-dox that Wakefield, whose propaganda gained its greatest successes with dissenting radicals whose ideas were the reverse of aristocratic, should have first stated his ideal in a form exactly confirming the developing pattern of the "pure merino" families of New South Wales and Van Diemen's Land.

By the 1830's, these families seemed to be established in the leadership of the older colonies, governing their economy and their politics as well as their society. Already they were build-ing the substantial stone houses so superbly drawn by Hardy Wilson in his *Old Colonial Architecture in New South Wales and Tasmania*,[16] houses which gave us an Indian summer of Georgian taste before the winter of domestic Victorian Gothic set in. Their numbers were increased by men of substance retiring from the East India Company or the British Army and attracted by climate as well as by commercial opportunity to the warmer Antipodes, men such as Charles Swanston,[17] the East India Company captain who set himself up in Hobart in 1831 as a banker and investor in pastoral ventures. Indeed, the providential merino, and its careful improvement, had turned miserable prisons into colonies which were fit and proper ob-jects of interest for men of station, men such as the Dumaresq brothers, products of the Royal Military College, who mi-grated to New South Wales when in 1825 their brother-in-law,

16. Sydney, 1924. See also his *The Cow Pasture Road* (Sydney, 1920).
17. S. J. Butlin, "Charles Swanston and the Derwent Bank, 1827–50," *Historical Studies, Australia and New Zealand*, II (1942–43), 161–85.

Sir Ralph Darling, was appointed Governor of that colony.[18]

It is true that there were some small clouds in their sunny skies. In his note to Commissioner Bigge, Macarthur had already lamented, "This democratic feeling [which] has taken deep root in the Colony, in consequence of the absurd and mischievous policy, pursued by Governor Macquarie," [19] an attribution grossly unjust to a great governor. The complaint of growing democracy continued; and indeed this was indirectly encouraged by the nature of their pastoral enterprises. For it is a quality of sheep-raising that, compared with agriculture and mining, it employs relatively few people where the wool is grown while it gives employment, directly and indirectly, to a relatively large number in the seaport town where its sale and despatch are managed. The shepherds and shearers, the fencers and sawyers and splitters, were few in comparison with those who worked in the warehouses and on the wharves of Sydney or Melbourne, or as clerks in the banks, the "loan and mercantile" companies and insurance offices which depended on wool for their business, to say nothing of those whose various occupations depended in a more indirect fashion on the prosperity of the colony's staple. The strangely urban emphasis of Australian development was evident early in its colonial history.

The seaport towns, Sydney, Hobart, Melbourne, and Adelaide, with their journalists and lawyers, their manufacturers and merchants, their shopkeepers and artisans, their market-gardeners and their labourers, their carters and their clerks, became the centres of varied and vocal political ideas which the substantial settlers too easily lumped together as democratic. The swelling entry of free immigrants, particularly after 1831 when the proceeds of land sales were used to assist them, added Irish discontent and Chartist idealism as uncomfortable leavens in the city mixture. Free immigrants were in any case

18. *The Australian Encyclopaedia* (1958), III, 308.
19. Clark, *Sources of Australian History*, p. 136.

less satisfactory than convicts to the landowners in the remoter districts because they were less subject to discipline and proved less willing to face the loneliness of the bush.

But the political agitation of the town itself was not always so democratic in aim as its emphatic eloquence in denunciation might make it appear. William Charles Wentworth, who dominated colonial politics between 1825 and 1854, had been described in 1830 by Governor Darling as a person "entirely excluded from Society, and his friends . . . in no better estimation with the respectable Classes of the Inhabitants than himself." ". . . the Character of Mr. Wentworth and his Associates," the Governor continued, "is too well known ever to permit of their having any influence except among individuals of the lowest Orders." [20] Yet, as A. C. V. Melbourne has shown, this offshoot of the great Fitzwilliam connection had always been dominated by the ideal of establishing a respectable lineage, and was not inconsistent in 1853 in advocating what would have amounted to a colonial House of Lords. In his youth, he had placed himself at the head of colonial agitation for self-government, using the uninhibited language of a man who thought in rhetoric; but he was not far out in his own later statement of his position, "I deny emphatically that I was ever a democrat or republican. I was a Whig, I admit, till I was ashamed of Whiggism. . . . At all events I shall die with conservative principles." [21] Urban radicalism was to be found more truly in such men as the Reverend John Dunmore Lang, the Scottish Presbyterian republican, and in Henry Parkes, Chartist, member of the Birmingham Political Union, and skilled artisan, who found himself redundant in overcrowded England and came to Sydney as an assisted immigrant, to become in time the outstanding political figure of his adopted colony, the most persistently caricatured but also the most widely respected.

20. Darling to Sir George Murray, 1 Dec. 1830, *Historical Records of Australia,* Series I, XV, 822.
21. Cited in *The Australian Encyclopaedia* (1958), IX, 243.

If the town increased, so did the number of those who might be relied upon to oppose its uncomfortable opinions; for these were the years, the 1830's and 1840's in particular, of the squatting movement, carried out in large measure by men whose ambition, however simple their beginnings, was to establish themselves as a landed gentry.

The earlier landowners had gained their estates by grant and by purchase; but land grants were ended by the Ripon regulations of 1831 while in the following years Wakefield's influence was to push up the minimum price at which crown land might be sold. Meanwhile, long experience of the cost of controlling and administering dispersed settlements had resulted, before Wakefield's influence could be felt, in a policy of restricting settlement within declared limits, which for New South Wales were "the nineteen counties" as delimited by Governor Darling in 1829. Even then, settlers were trespassing beyond the limits and during the 1830's as the settled districts filled up, pastoralists and their flocks ignored prohibitions and simply occupied crown lands beyond the limits in a vast wave of expansion which could neither be stopped nor ignored. Instead, the Governors, Bourke and Gipps, attempted to regulate it while protecting the rights of the crown, by allowing occupation, but no other right, in return for a license fee of ten pounds per annum and later a small tax on stock. The licence conferred no right of property nor any right or pre-emption; it allowed the squatter to squat legally for a year at a time so long as no one attempted to purchase his run. "As to evils of dispersion," declared Gipps in 1839, "I fear it is now too late to talk of them, for we have beyond the boundaries nearly two millions of sheep and several hundred thousands of cattle, which all the powers of Government could not bring back within the settled limits of the colony." [22]

The squatters could not be brought back because their industry was too valuable, both to the colony and Great

22. Cited by S. H. Roberts, *The Squatting Age in Australia, 1835–1847* (Melbourne University Press, 1935), p. 112.

Britain, and because they themselves were in general men of substance and some influence. Squatting was a highly capitalised business, as much an accompaniment of England's industrial expansion as a Yorkshire mill. It took several thousand pounds to establish a sheep run. Many of the squatters, it is true, had begun from scratch, but they were no longer penniless when they set up as squatters. John Robertson had saved £3,000 in nine years as an overseer in Tasmania before establishing himself as a pastoralist in Port Phillip. W. J. T. Clarke, later to become a millionaire, left Glastonbury in Somerset with nothing, but he could pay £2,931 for a right of run in Port Phillip in 1839 while maintaining properties in Tasmania. Sometimes smaller men combined, adding their savings of £500 or £600 each to the partnership. Many squatters were managing partners in companies which could invest a larger capital. For twenty years, George Russell, a Scottish farmer, managed Golf Hill for the Clyde Company which subscribed a capital of £16,000, £250,000 being distributed when the company was wound up.[23]

The first generation of squatters lived, as Gideon Scott Lang put it, "the same as their servants," [24] sparing nothing from their precious capital for ostentatious expenditure, nor even for comforts. But they worked to establish themselves in a life resembling that already achieved by the Macarthurs, the Bowmans, the Icelys, and others of the Camden set. The majority of them were Scots and, at that, Scots tenant farmers whose existing social status was less important than their determination to improve it. The English were more varied and numbered many an army officer or son of the rectory. Among the Irish were many who were already gentry, such as

23. These details are mostly derived from Miss Margaret Kiddle's still unpublished "Men of Yesterday." For George Russell and the Clyde Company, see P. L. Brown, ed., *The Narrative of George Russell of Golf Hill* (Oxford, 1935), pp. 365–66.

24. Gideon Scott Lang, *Land and Labour in Australia* (Melbourne, 1845), p. 12.

the Winters from County Meath who were to establish in
Victoria the cultured life which they could no longer preserve
in Ireland. Whatever their origins, the bark or slab or mud hut,
and the weatherboard cottage which succeeded it, were, if they
established themselves, mere stepping stones to the solid rural
mansions and the elegant town houses which they were building during the latter half of the century.

Such men were in the long run more important in establishing one of the patterns of Australian life than the few
speculators on a larger scale who had dabbled in pastoral opportunities, men like Benjamin Boyd, for example, a London
stockbroker, who came to Sydney in 1842, floated a bank,
established a whaling station, maintained a fleet of ships in
the Pacific trade, and held pastoral licences for, it seems, well
over two million acres of country. He was able to sway Lord
Stanley's land policy, but his vast empire faded with the failure
of his bank. Wentworth himself had engaged in pastoral
speculation of the same kind, holding fifteen pastoral runs
at one period, while his egregious agreement with the Maori
chieftains, properly disallowed by Gipps, would have given
him control over twenty million acres of New Zealand for
£200 a year.[25] But such ventures were exaggerations of a
movement of pastoral expansion which established in control
of large stretches of Eastern Australia a class of substantial
pastoralists who had in general no doubts either of their social
worth or of their natural claims to political leadership.

Their desire to gain security of tenure in those pastoral
holdings which they held only by licence or lease brought them
into active support of those older gentry who were now demanding self-government, a self-government in which they
assumed the natural leadership of a rural gentry. The rising
democracy of the towns was already opposing this assumption

25. See K. Buckley, "Gipps and the Graziers of New South Wales,
1841–46," *Historical Studies, Australia and New Zealand,* VI (1953–55),
396–412; VII (1956–57), 178–93.

and beginning the cry to wrest the pastoral lands from their control, when the discoveries of gold in New South Wales and Victoria brought in a flood of immigration which raised the population of the Australian colonies from 405,000 at the end of 1850, to 1,145,000 at the end of 1860, and that of Victoria from 77,000 to 540,000 during the same period.

It was in this decade, when all the social barriers seemed to be falling, that the colonies were allowed to draft their constitutions for self-government. In Sydney, Wentworth fought with all his eloquence and influence for "a constitution" —I quote his own words—"that will be a lasting one—a conservative one—a British, not a Yankee constitution. (Loud and prolonged cheers)," [26] and proposed, by the distribution of seats, the difficulty of amendment, and the provision of an upper house selected from the holders of inherited titles, to preserve the leadership of the men of estate. Against his will, Wentworth was himself in some degree responsible for the democratic amendment of his own constitution; for his plan was so exclusively designed to favour landed property that he drove the urban men of property, the merchants and manufacturers, into the arms of Sydney radicals in a common attack on a constitution designed for "Shepherd Kings." In any case, Lord John Russell was more liberal than Wentworth and removed his barrier against amendment. The local democrats, many of them men of property themselves, were not slow to amend his other restrictions out of existence. As he saw democracy swamping the barriers he had erected against it, the old battler was glad to depart. What could men of wealth aspire to in the colony, he had asked in defending his proposal for a hereditary upper house. "I will tell the Council: they aspire to a speedy migration to other lands ... where the democratic and levelling principles so rapidly increasing here

26. C. M. H. Clark, *Select Documents in Australian History, 1851–1900* (Sydney: Angus and Robertson, 1955), p. 336.

are scouted.... Who would stay here if he could avoid it?
Who with ample means would ever return?" [27]

By 1859, four Australian colonies enjoyed manhood suffrage
and four of them the secret ballot. And yet appearances were
deceptive. Unequal electorates protected rural interests, while
in several colonies plural voting and upper houses elected by
holders of property long imposed a barrier, by no means ineffec-
tive, to radical legislation. In Victoria, at least, the ideal of a
rural gentry had still to find its fullest expression in the landed
gentry of the Western District, while democracy stood, restive,
but often defeated, for a generation after the gold rushes. In
1873, Anthony Trollope described the "country gentlemen"
who "have built their houses with the English appurtenances
of substantial comfort, with many rooms, with gardens, out-
houses and lawns, and with sweeping roads leading through
timbered parks.... They or their fathers made their own
fortunes.... But," Trollope continued, "they now form an
established aristocracy, with very conservative feelings, and
are quickly becoming as firm a country party as that which is
formed by our squirarchy at home.... All those who frequent
the place are [the pastoralist's] servants or his guests, and of
every stranger whom he may see within miles of his house he
is entitled to ask why he is there. He exercises a wide hospitality to the poor and the rich, and he is an aristocrat." [28]

And yet, by that time they were "men of yesterday." Their
wealth was great, their social prestige unquestioned. Some of
them went beyond the prejudices of their class to a ripe
political wisdom, and a few, as we are now discovering from
their letters and their libraries, were men of taste and even of
some learning. But their rôle in politics remained merely
defensive as they manoeuvred to preserve their stake in the
country; and in the cultural life of the colonies their influence

27. Cited by Melbourne, *W. C. Wentworth*, pp. 86–87.
28. *Australia and New Zealand* (London, 1873), I, 465–66, 469.

was equally defensive and therefore equally negative. "Are not we all," wrote one of them in 1864, "Are not we all men of yesterday in various degree, the democrats of the day in all things having a majority? Is not this the beginning of Yankeedom stimulated by the golden Treasury in the earth we tread upon?" [29]

By the closing decade of the nineteenth century, most of the men who have been the subject of this lecture, the founders of Australia's pastoral aristocracy, were dead. "My compeers are dropping off very fast on every side of me," wrote Niel Black, who was one of them, in 1876, "and I sometimes begin to feel lonely." [30] Some of them had returned to England or Scotland to live the lives of retired country gentlemen in the counties which they had left forty or fifty years before; but most were too firmly rooted in Australian soil to leave it. A minority of the very successful had transformed themselves from pastoralists into financiers as they sought profitable investments for their savings. Most preferred to invest in the stock and land which were familiar to them, and so it came about in the sixties and seventies that Victorian money opened up the vast pastures of inland and tropical Queensland and of the Gulf Country. "Queensland is keeping half Toorak," it was said,[31] Toorak being the fashionable suburb of Melbourne in which the town houses of the great were to be found. But squatters' money went also into town allotments and woollen mills, and on a larger scale into the investment, banking and insurance companies which flourished in the boom of the 1880's. W. J. T. Clarke became "one of the directors of the Southern Insurance Company, the Colonial Bank and the National Bank," dying worth two and a half million pounds, i.e., ten or twelve million dollars; while Stephen Henty became an "importer and ship-

29. This extract from a letter from Niel Black to T. S. Gladstone, 1864, comes from Miss Margaret Kiddle's manuscript earlier referred to, and provides its title, "Men of Yesterday."

30. Letter to T. S. Gladstone, 3 August 1876, cited by Miss Kiddle.

31. Cited by Miss Kiddle.

ping broker, a director of the Colonial Life Assurance Company, a Commissioner of the Savings Bank, Chairman of the Southern Insurance Company and President of the City and Suburban Building Investment Company." [32] They, and those who merely retired from active management of their holdings, merged into the well-to-do society of Melbourne, scarcely to be distinguished from the judges and the physicians, the bankers and the merchants, who were their fellow members of the Melbourne Club.

At the other end of the scale were the pastoralists in difficulties. Economic historians have still to study their transformation; [33] but it is clear enough that the costs of acquiring the freehold of their stations and of defending their holdings against selectors, and the further costs of improvements—of fencing, of sowing pastures, of building substantial houses, even, in some cases, of sending their sons to Cambridge and their daughters to Paris—that these costs had reduced many of them to a dependence on banks and loan companies which turned some of them into the unsalaried managers rather than the owners of their estates. Certainly, to say nothing of overstocking and the consequent destruction of natural pastures, the indebtedness of many of the squatters left them defenceless in the bank crash of the 1890's when the twenty years fall in wool prices quickened and could no longer be concealed by renewed borrowing.

But those who faced this crisis were the sons, and they were a different race of men. Their fathers, 70 per cent of them Scots, had been gentlemen by ambition and achievement, but not by origin. For their sons they had willed an easier life, and sometimes regretted the results. These young men might feel themselves defiantly Australian in Oxford or Cambridge where

32. M. Kiddle.
33. But see N. G. Butlin, "Company Ownership of N.S.W. Pastoral Stations, 1865–1900," *Historical Studies, Australia and New Zealand,* IV (1949–51), 89–111.

they were sent, not for what Niel Black called "mere education" which they could get in Melbourne, but in order "to
enlarge their views and knowledge of mankind on a wider
field of observation"; [34] but the polish they had been sent to
acquire separated them from their fathers, and perhaps made
the latter the more reluctant even in their old age to allow the
management of properties they had wrested from the wilderness to slip into the unpractised hands of those who were to
succeed them. Certainly, Niel Black was not alone in com-
plaining of "the fast, flash doings" of those who had completed
their university education at Oxford or Cambridge and, having
nothing to do, went in as he put it for "horse racing and fast
doings." [35] In so far as that was a just accusation and not merely
the older generation begrudging the younger its youth, those
who made the accusation bore a large share of responsibility
for its truth. The majority probably of the second generation
settled down in time to the management of their inherited
estates; but yet their rôle in the government and the culture of
the country bore no adequate relation to their importance in
its economy. They did not provide a governing class, and even
their strength in the upper houses declined as the century drew
towards its end. It was not they, but the lawyers and journalists
and self-made businessmen of the cities who provided the
colonies with political leaders. It may be true that although
defensively Australian in England, they seemed Englishmen in
Australia, uprooted from the land of their birth and yet living
in it—in it, but perhaps not altogether of it, living reserved and
remote from the brash democracy that was growing up about
them. Perhaps their failure to participate in its shaping has
more to do with the twenty years struggle from 1860 between
squatters and selectors; for if the selection laws, some of which
at least seemed to have been designed rather to ruin the
squatters than to place farmers on the land, had left the

34. N. Black, 9 July 1879, cited by Miss Kiddle.
35. N. Black to T. S. Gladstone, 25 March 1872, cited by Miss Kiddle.

squatters resentful of a wholesale attack on them as a class, their readiness—their inevitable and successful readiness—to use all the means which legal chicanery and their bank credit opened to them to defeat those laws had left them with lowered prestige and reduced influence.

Nor, despite magnificent exceptions, did they compensate for their relative withdrawal from political leadership by any general support of the arts and learning. My own University of Melbourne owes a College, a ceremonial hall, and two Chairs to the generosity of pastoralists; and other Australian universities can offer similar evidence to serve as a caution against underestimating the pastoralists' contribution. But it remains difficult to avoid the conclusion that in culture as in politics the majority held aloof from the new society that was being shaped so vociferously about them. They were indeed "men of yesterday," and the future that was then being moulded was not moulded in their image.

II

The Birth of a Culture

To visitors from older countries, the society of the Australian colonies in the late nineteenth century presented a brash, unfinished, and boastful front, above all in Victoria. South Australia was quieter. Succeeding Tasmania in the fifties as the granary of Australia, it had balanced the wealth of its squatters by the prosperity of its farmers, while its politics had with scarcely a ripple been dominated by the self-respecting radical dissenters who had been attracted by the idealistic strands in Wakefield's schemes. Tasmania and West Australia languished until the mining booms near the end of the century. New South Wales, not deeply changed by its gold rushes, continued a steady pace of development that seemed stagnation only beside the mushroom growth of its southern neighbour. Queensland, newest of the colonies, was still in the first stage of pioneering, fed, whether for cattle stations or sugar plantations, by Victorian capital. But Victoria, only fifteen years old when gold was discovered, had been transformed by the gold rushes of the 1850's into not only the most populous but also the most complex and most highly urbanised of the colonies. Numbering almost as many people as those of all the other Australian colonies combined, Victorians in 1861 needed no reminder for themselves of the speed and splendour of their achievement, but they were always ready to remind anyone else,

> Loud-voiced and reckless as the wild tide-race
> That whips our harbour mouth.[1]

1. "The Song of the Cities. Melbourne."

That was Kipling's description in 1893 when in fact the bank crash had quietened any remaining tendency of Victorians to blow. Trollope had been nearer the truth twenty years earlier when he wrote in his *Australia and New Zealand:* "They blow a good deal in Queensland;—a good deal in South Australia. They blow even in poor Tasmania. They blow loudly in New South Wales and very loudly in New Zealand. But the blast of the trumpet as heard in Victoria is louder than all the blasts— and the Melbourne blast beats all the other blowing of that proud colony." [2] It is a judgment that sounds strangely in the ears of a twentieth-century Australian, more accustomed to hearing that Melbourne is English, conservative, cautious, hiding its virtues—all terms used as synonyms—while Sydney is American, experimental, brash, flaunting its facades—again, all terms used as synonyms. Yet both the nineteenth-century judgment and the twentieth-century reversal of it can · be voluminously documented, while the changes of today are robbing such stereotypes of meaning and value.

The progress of which Victorians boasted had made Melbourne by 1901 a large city, of the same general order of magnitude at that time as Munich and Milan, or as Baltimore and Boston. "Melbourne," wrote Francis Adams in 1886, "has what might be called, the *metropolitan tone.* The look on the faces of her inhabitants is the *metropolitan look.* These people live quickly; such as life presents itself to them, they know it: as far as they can see, they have no prejudices." [3] In less spectacular fashion but backed by more extensive natural resources, New South Wales was by the end of the century overhauling Victoria in numbers and in the scale of its economic effort, and was exhibiting the same urban concentration of its people. The Australia that was formed into a Commonwealth by the federation of the six colonies in 1901 was not yet

2. London, 1873, I, 387.
3. *Australian Essays,* pp. 1 ff., cited in M. Clark, *Sources of Australian History* (Oxford University Press, 1957), p. 453.

the highly industrialised society of today; but it was already, in size, in variety of livelihood, and in the unusual concentration of its people in cities, outgrowing its colonial swaddling-clothes.

In the preceding half-century, its 400,000 people had increased to close on 4,000,000, at a rate unsurpassed elsewhere. This growing population had equipped itself with 13,000 miles of railway; after much misdirected effort, it had extended its cultivated land from under half a million acres to close on ten million; it had increased the number of its sheep from 17,000,-000 to a peak of 106,000,000 in 1891; it had established a variety of industries, most of them on a small scale still, and had built some large cities. Fed until 1890 by an impressive rate of immigration and by continued investment from Great Britain, it had increased the national output (although not the output per head) at a rate second only to that of the United States. Resounding bank crashes in the early 1890's and disastrous droughts had checked this progress; but the studies of N. G. Butlin and his associates at the Australian National University have shown that recovery was rapid and that the lost ground had been recovered by 1900, despite continuing drought.[4]

The most striking feature of this half-century of development was the increasing concentration of people in towns, so that by 1901, 41 per cent of Victorians lived in Melbourne while 35 per cent of the people of New South Wales lived in Sydney.

"The progress of the chief cities of Australasia," wrote T. A. Coghlan in 1902, "has been remarkable, and has no parallel among the cities of the old world. Even in America the rise of the great cities has been accompanied by a corresponding increase in the rural population, but in Australia, perhaps for

4. See N. G. Butlin, *Public Capital Formation in Australia: Estimates 1861–1900* and *Private Capital Formation in Australia: Estimates 1861–1900*, Social Science Monographs Nos. 2 and 5 (Australian National University, 1955); and "The Shape of the Australian Economy, 1861–1900," *Economic Record*, XXXIV (1958), 10–29.

the first time in history, was presented the spectacle of magnificent cities growing with marvellous rapidity, and embracing within their limits one-third of the population of the states of which they are the seat of governments. The abnormal aggregation of the population into their capital cities is a most unfortunate element in the progress of these states, and as regards some of them, is becoming more marked every year." [5] So true has Coghlan's concluding remark continued to be that today more than half of all Australians live in half-a-dozen capital cities.

The temper of the society which built these cities and the railways which connected them was democratic, and so were its achievements. The manhood suffrage and secret ballot achieved in most of the Australian colonies in the 1850's had long been held in check by propertied upper houses, by plural voting, and by an unequal distribution of electorates. The seeming social advances which followed had similar limits, for the eight-hour day, first achieved in 1856, was the privilege of a few skilled trades, and the land laws of the sixties had not succeeded in providing homesteads for the people. "By contrast," and I quote Professor Manning Clark, whose criticism of the "spiritual and cultural mediocrity" of this later period I wish to examine, "By contrast, the legislation of the second period (1880–1900) did touch the core of political privilege, and forced the men of property to accept the idea that all should enjoy a measure of material well-being. The abolition of plural voting, payment of members, and votes for women went a long way towards making political equality a reality. The social legislation passed by some of the parliaments—graduated income taxes, graduated land taxes, graduated death duties, and the cautious system of old age pensions in New South Wales and Victoria—was the price the new democracy exacted from the old order. Nor was this all. True, the parlia-

5. T. A. Coghlan, *A Statistical Account of the Seven Colonies of Australasia, 1901–2* (Sydney: Government Printer, 1902), p. 543.

ments ran away from the radical demand that the State should regulate hours of work, wages, and working conditions. But they were prepared to prescribe maximum hours for women, and ban child labour, and," he concludes, "at least three of the colonies flirted coyly with the idea of a minimum wage for all by establishing Wages Boards in a limited number of trades." [6]

These changes were brought about with relative ease in a society which was familiar with change of status and which, as Higinbotham put it, had relatively few paupers and no "dangerous class." [7] Even Australian conservatives shared the liberal optimism in the later years of the century when the old landowners were dead and the new relatively inactive in politics; and it was a Victorian conservative, James Service, who stated the axiomatic belief of Australian politics, irrespective of party, "that every man should start fair in life, and have the same chance of making his way through the world." [8]

In the closing years of the century when the colonies were forming the Commonwealth of Australia, an exuberant optimism frequently transformed that sober principle into an inflated expectation of an antipodean paradise. It is difficult to separate actual belief from the flowing rhetoric inseparable from the inauguration of a new Commonwealth; but the Brisbane *Worker*'s comments on that occasion—expressed at such length as to suggest that amplitude of rhetoric went in inverse proportion to substance—only echoed views that were widely held. The nation, declared the *Worker*,

cradled and nurtured by Democrats, must if it is true to itself remain, even become more, Democratic. . . . And this is Australia's manifest destiny if she is to fulfil any nobler destiny than the nations decayed and decaying. She may be a rich nation collectively, composed of a

6. C. M. H. Clark, *Select Documents in Australian History, 1851–1900* (Sydney: Angus and Robertson, 1955), pp. xii–xiii.

7. Edward Wilson, *An Enquiry into the Principles of Representation* (Melbourne, 1857), p. 21.

8. *Victorian Parliamentary Debates*, Vol. 59, p. 2581.

horde of individual paupers. She may be grand and great and glorious, with teeming slums of criminals. She may have Universities and Academies and Salons, yet her people may be ignorant and vicious. She may expand her territories and leave her home provinces ill-governed, conquer other peoples while her own are in revolt, show a substantial front to the world while all within is rotten and corrupt. By following the precept and example of the older nations she may easily accomplish all these things, for is she not young and strong and vigorous? Never has a nation before been launched under such happy auspices, but so complex and various are the ideas of statesmanship that Australia may be wrecked unless the true ideal—the ideal which should be the guiding star of her destiny—is kept in sight.

. . . .

And this ideal, though not so large, and airy, and grandiloquent, as glory, and wealth, and conquest, is a basic one; and withal is so simple that anyone can comprehend it. It is the state built up of a multitude of perfect human units. The perfect whole, composed as it must necessarily be, of perfect parts. This is the ideal of the Labour Democrats whose aim is to pass measures for the purpose not of making fortunes or becoming famous, but to give a full, complete, and happy life to the people. To make existence light and happiness attainable and the government really the protector and fosterer of the people. The Old Order has failed; this is the New! Which destiny is Australia to fulfil? [9]

Naturally differences soon appeared when such vague affirmations of faith were translated into programmes of action; but the political and social achievement of those years should warn us against merely dismissing even such bombast as the leader I have just quoted. A later generation of Australians has not failed to criticize the shortcomings of the faith of this generation of their grandfathers. It is true that their ideal on its negative side was exclusive and even intolerant, and that it often degenerated into a prejudice that one finds painful to reconstruct, as when the *Bulletin* in 1893, declaring itself in favour of "Australia for the Australians," underlined its mean-

---

9. *The Worker* (Brisbane), 5 Jan. 1901, cited in M. Clark, *Sources of Australian History*, pp. 467–70.

ing with the explanation, "The cheap Chinaman, the cheap nigger, and the cheap European pauper to be absolutely excluded." [10] It is also true that experience has not established the nobler belief of such liberals as Higgins and Deakin that material progress would be followed inevitably by spiritual and moral progress, although it is not thereby demonstrated that they were wrong in seeking to end sordid poverty and petty oppression, in which spiritual and moral depravity certainly flourish. It is true that many of them were unaware of the checks imposed on their hopes both by the natural limits of an arid environment and by the troubled world outside, that is, by history. Professor Clark's apocalyptic vision goes further and leaves him "dumbfounded at their optimism, astounded that belief in material progress and mateship could be their only comforters against earth and sky, man and beast." [11] It is for the prophet rather than the historian to take a generation that is dead to task for failing, as it did fail, to see the signs of the apocalypse about it; and even for the prophet it is more useful to speak, as indeed Professor Clark really intends, to the generation that is living, the generation which he regards, I expect, as the children whose teeth are set on edge.

I have, indeed, much sympathy for his vision and for his readiness to point to the shallowness of shibboleths that have too often done service for thought with us. But for that earlier generation it will be both more just and more profitable to understand rather than to judge; and understanding may illuminate the problem to which this sketch of the social setting has been leading: namely, what are the conditions which delay and those which at length allow the creation in a new society of a literature and an art, of a mature science and scholarship? Some characteristics of that generation were not peculiar to Australia. The decline of religious belief, which Professor Clark

10. 17 Jan. 1893, cited in M. Clark, *Sources of Australian History*, p. 447.
11. C. M. H. Clark, *Select Documents*, p. xv.

and others have deplored, was characteristic of the age elsewhere and not only in Australia, even if it accorded with some
spiritual thinness in colonial life. And a Philistine tyranny of
the majority—surely too often and too easily called on for ex-
cuse by some of our writers and scholars—might be, as many
from Jacob Burckhardt's day to this have believed, a quality of
industrial democracy in general and not merely of Australian
society in particular. But it remains true, independently of
these things, that colonial history normally shows for some
time a poverty in the things of the mind. This does not make
it uninteresting; indeed, it may have an intense interest for
social and economic historians, for anthropologists, demog-
raphers, political scientists, and many others. But its interest
is of a different kind, and if you seek those who have made
original and fundamental contributions to the world's thought
or art or literature or science, you must look, with some brilliant exceptions, outside the colonial phase of Australian history. This truth is not confined to the colonial history of Australia. "The Canadian public," wrote a Canadian writer, "is
ignorant, cowardly and snobbish. It is mortally afraid of ideas
and considers the discussion of fresh principles as a betrayal
of bad manners." "Canada is a non-conductor for any sort of
intellectual current." [12] I owe these extracts to a Canadian,
Professor C. T. Bissell of Toronto, and use them to suggest that
intellectual and artistic thinness may be a common quality in
modern colonial development.

It was not that colonists lacked capacity, nor even that they
entirely lacked some initial encouragement. Samuel Alexander,
the "English" philosopher, was born in Sydney in 1859 and
received his early education in Melbourne at Wesley College
and the University, where he distinguished himself in a company of no mean competitors. But this future president of the
Aristotelian Society, Fellow of the British Academy, and first

12. F. P. Grove, *In Search of Myself,* as quoted by C. T. Bissell in a
public lecture in Melbourne.

of the three Australians to be awarded the rare Order of Merit, could not have done in Melbourne at that time the work which brought him fame. It might seem, however, that the reasons which may be offered for this conclusion—isolation from the main centres of thought, lack of a sufficient number of equal competitors in the same field, and the few and scattered opportunities for intellectual livelihood—need not explain the delayed flowering of a native literature, the spirit blowing where it listeth. Literature and the arts do indeed present special problems, their difficulties being not quite the same as those which hindered the full growth of science and other learning. The universities with which Sydney and Melbourne had provided themselves in the 1850's offered a sound training, and the growth of literary and scientific scholarship required only an extension of such opportunities and a more varied and sophisticated society to nourish it. But literature and art, if they were to put down local roots, required revolt.

The derivative culture which was purveyed to their pupils by the Sydney College and by Scotch College and Wesley in Melbourne, and that which was, with improving zeal, offered to the working classes in the Mechanics' Institutes and Schools of Arts founded to temper colonial materialism, this culture could nourish in literature polite accomplishments, but it could not by itself nourish an indigenous art. The writer needed to be free of his environment, to be able to see it, whether it were his human or his natural environment, with fresh eyes, his vision no longer blurred by the irrelevant images of another world. He needed to go beyond Kendall's apology for the Australian birds who "Sing in September their songs of the Maytime." [13]

The closing decades of the old century and the opening decade of this saw the creation of the first distinctively Australian literature, one which was neither mature nor in universal terms

13. An observation which I owe to Dr. R. B. Ward, *The Australian Legend* (Melbourne: Oxford University Press, 1958), p. 203.

great, but one, nevertheless, which achieved this emancipation and thereby made possible a continuing development beyond its own limitations.

The achievement of the writers in discovering Australia was paralleled by the plein-air painters who in the eighties and nineties made themselves freemen of the Australian scene, evolved the higher tonal palette its light required, and raised their flag of revolt in the "9 by 5 Exhibition of Impressions" which was held in Melbourne in August, 1889. "Of the 180 exhibits catalogued on the present occasion," wrote James Smith in the Melbourne *Argus*, "four-fifths are a pain to the eye.... There are landscapes and samples of architecture, belonging to some embryotic world, in which, as Pandulph says, 'All form is formless, order orderless,' and nature herself is either unshapen or misshapen.... A few [of the sketches] afford something agreeable to the eye to rest upon, but the exhibition, viewed as a whole, would leave a very painful feeling behind it, and cause one to despond with respect to the future of art in this colony, did we not believe with M. W. P. Frith, R.A., that 'Impressionism is a craze of such ephemeral character as to be unworthy of serious attention.' " [14] The elegant and, indeed, skilled confidence of this review gives one some measure of the weight of imported convention. One is tempted to pursue the subject, asking how far the local revolt had any special character differentiating it from the general impressionist revolt against academic tradition. But the problems with which I am concerned are more clearly presented in the literature of this time, and to that I return.

At a time when Australians were already congregating in a few large cities, this literature was a literature of the outback, and at a time when the outback still preserved an oligarchic or even aristocratic structure, it was strongly democratic. Neither its democratic nor its rural quality need surprise us. Those

14. Cited in James Grant and Geoffrey Serle, *The Melbourne Scene, 1803–1956* (Melbourne University Press, 1957), pp. 182–83.

whose views were conservative did not write a literature of revolt, and those who did write it were not on the whole people who were at ease in the best society. But in trying to shake themselves free of a tradition which they felt to be alien, conservative and cramping, those writers at the end of the century who were writing in an assertively Australian fashion turned eagerly from the town, which seemed to be secondhand and European, to the outback which offered them the most distinctively Australian types of life and scene to be found on the continent. And among the bush-workers of the outback they found a tradition of irreverence towards authority and of loyalty towards one's fellows which appealed to their own radical instincts. This bush tradition was turned into a legend by the Sydney weekly, *The Bulletin*. Archibald, its editor, made up his mind to shock his society out of its complacency. "It was a cant-ridden community," he wrote in retrospect,

Cant—the offensive, horrible cant of the badly-reformed sinner—reigned everywhere. There was no health in the public spirit socially and politically; all was a mean subservience to a spirit of snobbery and dependency. What was most Australian in spirit had been lost by the secession first of Victoria, and then of Queensland. Sydney socially limped in apish imitation after London ideas, habits, and manners. Politically and industrially it was the same. And over all brooded, in law courts, press and Parliament, the desolating cruelty inherited from "The System." Sydney invited revolt from the existing conditions, and the *Bulletin* was the organ of that revolt. It was to stand for more humanity in the laws, more freedom in the Parliament, more healthy independence in the press.[15]

As Miss Ailsa G. Thomson has shown,[16] the *Bulletin* was not the first to exploit the rich vein of outback Australia as a means of exposing what were felt to be the shams and cant of the city, limping apishly behind its European models. But its "exuberant and irreverent radicalism, its outspoken attack on all local

15. Cited in Vance Palmer, *National Portraits* (Sydney: Angus and Robertson, 1940), p. 125.
16. "The Early History of the *Bulletin*," *Historical Studies, Australia and New Zealand*, VI (1954), 121–34.

brands of hypocrisy, and the quick parry and thrust of its new journalistic style gained it a widening circle of readers until it became not merely a local but a national paper." [17] The *Bulletin* did, indeed, play an unequalled rôle in shaping this new Australian literature. At a time when roughly four in five Australians were native born, were those who had no nostalgic memories of green English fields, it made them aware of their country, and encouraged its readers to write for it their tales of the outback and of the life lived in it. Its contributors included the writers who did most to create a distinctive literature at this time, Henry Lawson, Joseph Furphy, Bernard O'Dowd, and many others.

In its deliberate irreverence, the *Bulletin* was sometimes silly and often unfair. The silliness was balanced in time when A. G. Stephens in his "Red Page" brought to bear on Australian writing, standards of criticism formed by a wide reading in European literature. The unfairness was inevitable: a revolt against convention is unlikely to succeed if it is beset by anxiety to be fair to the thing attacked, nor are those who are anxious to be fair likely to lead a revolt. But it taught Australian writers to write directly and in their own idiom, and its own constant example of exuberant irony suited that idiom. "The Sermon on the Mount," declared a *Bulletin* leader during the Boer War which it opposed, "is publicly suspended as a beautiful theory that doesn't suit the times and the circumstances." [18] That same veneer of irony concealing a raw and sensitive idealism is clear in the best novel of this phase of Australian writing, Joseph Furphy's *Such is Life*. "The successful pioneer is the man who never spared others, the forgotten pioneer is the man who never spared himself, but being a fool, built homes for wise men to live in, and omitted to gather moss." [19]

In the bush, then, the *Bulletin* writers found a tradition

17. R. M. Crawford, "The Australian National Character: Myth and Reality," *Journal of World History*, II (1955), 716.

18. 10 Feb. 1900.

19. Tom Collins (Joseph Furphy), *Such Is Life* (2nd ed.; Melbourne, 1917), p. 86.

which seemed to combine both their idealism and their irony; for the nomadic bush-workers—the shearers who moved from station to station in close-knit parties, the fencers and splitters, the trappers, the boundary-riders, and bullock-drivers, those, in short, who congregated in "the men's quarters" and not in "the homestead"—presented a cohesive loyalty to each other and an independence and irreverence for authority which answered the *Bulletin's* book. Francis Adams had found the bush-workers "the one powerful and unique national type yet produced in Australia. . . . This contains," he declared, "the *fons et origo* of the New Race." [20]

Dr. Russell Ward has explored the origins of this tradition in convict days,[21] its preservation by the circumstances of the bush, its expression in the bush ballads, and its impact, by way of the Shearers' Unions and the pages of *The Bulletin*, on Australian labour. The rebellious sentiment of many of the bush ballads which he uses as evidence had its origin in an Ireland that was far away and in resentment of a convict discipline that was long past; and when bush-workers of a later day sang the bush-ranging ballads, they were expressing merely a general habit of independence rather than a particular disposition towards rebellion.

> Then come all my hearties we'll roam the mountains high,
> Together we will conquer, together we will die.
> We'll wander over mountains, we'll gallop over plains,
> For we scorn to live in slavery, bound down by iron chains.

As Dr. Ward has shown, the solidarity of the nomad tribe is the theme common to all these ballads. And in all the writing inspired by the bush legend and by the ballads which expressed it, this loyalty to one's fellows is presented as a virtue to be taken for granted. It was, indeed, a loyalty made necessary by the dangers of the bush and extended by its loneliness

20. Francis Adams, *The Australians: A Social Sketch* (London: T. Fisher Unwin, 1893), p. 163.
21. *The Australian Legend.*

beyond one's human companions. "That there dog," said Macquarie the shearer in Henry Lawson's story, *That There Dog of Mine*, "is a better dog than I'm a man . . . and a better Christian. He's been a better mate to me than I ever was to any man—or any man to me." Henry Lawson was a short-story writer of rare quality; of him as a poet it is best to say little except that the bush-ballad jingle was adequate for the simple sentiments of his rhymes. It is in one of these, "The Shearers," that the much discussed doctrine of mateship received its clearest statement:

> No church-bell rings them from the Track
> No pulpit lights their blindness.
> 'Tis hardship, drought, and homelessness
> That teach those Bushmen kindness:
> The mateship born in barren lands,
> Of toil and thirst and danger,
> The campfire for the wanderer set,
> The first place to the stranger.
>
> .   .   .   .   .   .
>
> They tramp in mateship side by side—
> The Protestant and Roman—
> They call no biped lord or sir,
> And touch their hat to no man!

We need not wonder why the 30 per cent of Australians who lived in the capital cities read a bush literature and even thought of themselves in its terms. The bush was romantic, while the town was their place of daily routine. So Frank Wilmot, one of the few Australian poets of the town in the past generation, could write:

> Why didn't somebody say before I was old
> That there were brumbies to break and these store
>   mobs to muster
> When I was bred to the clang of a tram bell,
> Answered an 'ad' and took up a shopman's duster? [22]

22. "The Agricultural Show, Flemington, Victoria," in *Poems by Furnley Maurice (Frank Wilmot)*, selected by Percival Serle (Melbourne: Lothian Publishing Co., 1944).

But it is a little more puzzling to understand the completeness with which the bush legend of the *Bulletin* writers, with its elements of mateship, independence and irreverence towards traditional authority, established itself as the Australian self-picture, as the way even town-dwelling Australians saw themselves and have continued to see themselves, so that even in 1950 a Melbourne newspaper could speak of "the real, typical Australians outside the capital cities." It is less difficult to understand why Australian writers were so slow to come to grips with the life of the city. Perception of the imaginative possibilities of the city required a higher level of sophistication than was usual in Australian towns in 1900, and it was not until the 1930's that our novelists turned more than rarely to urban themes. At that, it was in most cases merely a transfer to an urban setting of the traditional bush literature's interest in the workers, the displaced persons, the outcasts of society. Whether the scene were the bush tracks or a slum tenement, the theme was the same, the nobility to be found in unexpected places. But the more subtle thoughts of the educated imposed tougher demands on writers and had to await increase of sophistication in our society. It is a sign of that increase that Australian writers are turning, and with at least a professional facility, to urban themes, and there is a world of change between Furphy's *Such is Life*, published in 1902, and Seaforth Mackenzie's *The Refuge*, published half a century later in 1954.

The Canadian parallel again reminds us that reluctance to explore the life of the city is not a peculiarity of Australian writing. Of the Canadian novel, Professor Bissell has said, "It is significant that most of our novels have a rural setting: imaginatively we have yet to acknowledge our urban status. Our novelists have many of the bucolic virtues: they have as yet acquired only a few of the urban sophistications." [23] In the Australian case, the dominance of the bush in the literature of the turn of the century had a special additional cause. Almost

23. In a lecture given in Melbourne.

all Australian towns of any size clung to the seacoast, and inland stretched the bush in its immensity to dominate the imagination.

In any case, the bush tradition as interpreted by the *Bulletin* writers answered to the imaginative needs of the townspeople. Their nationalism, their sense of an independent identity as Australians, was best expressed by the presentation of that Australia which seemed most distinctive, and the idealistic strand that was woven into that presentation answered to their own idealism. The belief that Australia might yet build a society free of the inequalities and injustices of the old world was widely held, even when the possible failure of this hope was admitted. "My own particular vision of Australia," said O'Dowd, "is something like this. She is an entity with a new destiny—if she wills it. She is the fabled Astraea Redux, the Goddess of Justice returning to earth as in the Golden Age when Saturn sojourned with us: that is, if she wills it. If not why simply Europe with its aura of failure over again, with perhaps a tinge of colour added for variety, and—new woes!" [24] The belief that this choice was open operated strongly in town and country and among people of all classes; and liberals from Henry Parkes to Deakin could always appeal to it with success. The more conservative found it easy to drop the elements of revolt in the bush tradition and to retain its vague idealism. The manifestations of Australian nationalism at this time have yet to be fully explored; but it is clear that a strong national feeling was by no means the monopoly of the republican and socialist minorities, and that as the separate colonies formed the Commonwealth of Australia at the close of the century, it was just as strong in many far more respectable groups.

Radical or conservative, Bohemian or respectable, they agreed in finding the most distinctive assertion of Australia's separate identity to be its life of the bush. And the literary

24. Cited by Vance Palmer, *The Legend of the Nineties* (Melbourne University Press, 1954), p. 120.

achievement of the exploration of this life by the *Bulletin* and other writers was that it gave Australians the freedom of their country, put the keys to it in their hands. The cities could wait a generation for a more complex, more sophisticated stage of our history. The first task, if there was to be an Australian literature, was to master a physical setting which had not yet been tamed by any familiar images.

For indeed there was a literary hurdle to be surmounted. Its nature may be seen in the work of Marcus Clarke, whose novel, *His Natural Life*,[25] was the first Australian novel to be widely read outside Australia. It remains one of the few of which that can be said. Marcus Clarke arrived in Melbourne from England in 1862 and became the centre of its first literary circle, the Yorick Club. In his novel nature stands as a fitting backdrop to his grim and powerfully written drama of convict life, a stage setting that matches its brooding despair; but it is theatrical, literary, and unreal. The rain-soaked forest of Macquarie Harbour, the sombre grandeur of Port Arthur, these are magnificent, but they are also foreign and strange.

That same sense of a landscape looked at from the outside is clear in a later preface written by Marcus Clarke to Adam Lindsay Gordon's poems. "What is the dominant note of Australian scenery?" he asks, and goes on to answer:

That which is the dominant note of Edgar Allan Poe's poetry— Weird Melancholy. A poem like "L'Allegro" could never be written by an Australian. It is too airy, too sweet, too freshly happy. The Australian mountain forests are funereal, secret, stern. Their solitude is desolation. They seem to stifle, in their black gorges, a story of sullen despair. No tender sentiment is nourished in their shade. In other lands the dying year is mourned, the falling leaves drop lightly on his bier. In the Australian forests no leaves fall. The savage winds shout among the rock clefts. From the melancholy gum, strips of

25. This first appeared in serial form in the *Australian Journal* from March 1870, and as a book, with some changes, in 1874, under the title *His Natural Life*, published as *For the Term of his Natural Life* by Angus and Robertson, Sydney, in 1929.

white bark hang and rustle. The very animal life of these frowning hills is either grotesque or ghostly. Great grey kangaroos hop noiselessly over the coarse grass. Flights of white cockatoos stream out, shrieking like evil souls. The sun suddenly sinks, and the mopokes burst out into horrible peals of semi-human laughter. . . . All is fear-inspiring and gloomy. No bright fancies are linked with the memories of the mountains. Hopeless explorers have named them out of their sufferings—Mount Misery, Mount Dreadful, Mount Despair. As when among sylvan scenes in places made green with the running of rivers, and gracious with temperate air, the soul is soothed and satisfied, so, placed before the frightful grandeur of these barren hills, it drinks in their sentiment of defiant ferocity, and is steeped in bitterness. . . . But the dweller in the wilderness acknowledges the subtle charm of this fantastic land of monstrosities. He becomes familiar with the beauty of loneliness . . . and the Poet of our desolation begins to comprehend why free Esau loved his heritage of desert sand better than all the bountiful richness of Egypt.[26]

I am indeed aware that I have left the stern discipline of my professed trade far behind and plead the licence of an occasional lecture which may be allowed to encourage a more speculative reflection. Clarke's work was brilliant and there it stopped. A native literature could grow only when the native scene became more than the outlandish occasion for a theatrical literary emotion, became—both the scene and the life lived in it—the accepted and familiar daily fare. It was the achievement of this self-consciously Australian period of our literature that it gave our writers—and indeed their readers—that sense of being at ease with their world. Even when they are describing the "harsh Biblical country of the scapegoat," [27] a theme that might easily breed theatrical writing, the generation of writers who were tutored in the bush tradition, wore it easily, like an old coat. So in his story of a young English clergyman in the drought-stricken outback, Dowell O'Reilly is content to

26. Preface to Adam Lindsay Gordon, *Poems* (Melbourne: A. H. Massina and Co., 1894).
27. Judith Wright, "The Remittance Man," in *The Moving Image* (Melbourne: Meanjin Press, 1946).

let an impression convey the rising dust-storm, and to let rhetoric take care of itself: "He turned his back to the wind that
licked the baked soil bare as concrete. The heavier particles,
driving along the ground, tinkled against the steel spokes, and
piled to windward of the tyres. He moved his foot, and already
its outline was ridged in dust. He looked at it curiously, re-
membering the strange heaps of red earth against the western
side of every post." [28]

In time, not without warnings which still continue lest we
turn Australian literature into "a vast geographical cliché," the
scene could even be taken for granted, and our literature could
begin, as it has now begun, to add maturity to its undoubted
vigour.

Familiarity did not breed contempt, nor did a confirmed
habit of pricking the bubbles of pretentiousness prevent the
incurable idealist that the Australian is, even in his frequent
moments of acidulous irony, from discovering in the familiar
things the "symbols of the Spirit's vaster span." [29] And as that
generation of writers mastered its environment, the crude uto-
pianism which had so stirred them was transmuted by some
of their successors into a more subtle faith, as in Judith Wright's
poem, "The Bullocky":

> Beside his heavy-shouldered team,
> thirsty with drought and chilled with rain,
> he weathered all the striding years
> till they ran widdershins in his brain:
>
> Till the long solitary tracks
> etched deeper with each lurching load
> were populous before his eyes
> and fiends and angels used his road.

28. "Crows," in *Australian Short Stories* (Oxford University Press, The
World's Classics, 1951), p. 147.

29. "The Towers at Evening," in *Poems by Furnley Maurice* (*Frank
Wilmot*), selected by Percival Serle (Melbourne: Lothian Publishing Co.,
1944).

All the'long straining journey grew
a mad apocalyptic dream,
and he old Moses; and his slaves
his suffering and stubborn team.

Then in his evening camp beneath
the half-light pillars of the trees
he filled the steepled cone of night
with shouted prayers and prophecies,

While past the campfire's crimson ring
the star-struck darkness cupped him round
and centuries of cattle-bells
rang with their sweet uneasy sound.

Grass is across the waggon-tracks
and plough strikes bone beneath the grass,
and vineyards cover all the slopes
where the dead teams were used to pass.

O vine grow close upon that bone
and hold it with your rooted hand.
The Prophet Moses feeds the grape
and fruitful is the Promised Land.[30]

This was the maturity of the bush tradition. In its earlier stages, most writing in this tradition had been amateurish. The verse was vigorous, prolific, and at times lyrical; the prose, better on the whole, realistic and salty. But professional work, to be praised not for its promise but for its achievement, was rare. And in this it was true to the society of that time. Professional standards result only from a full-time devotion to the mastery of one's craft; and the Australian society of that time, utilitarian in the choice of purposes to which wealth might be devoted, gave only rare opportunities for a professional life in literature, or even for that matter in scholarship. The painters could precariously attempt to live by painting; but they went overseas if they could, seeking wider opportunity as well as wider stimulus. The journalists, lawyers, shopkeepers and pub-

30. In *The Moving Image.*

lic servants who wrote in their spare time could rarely produce work of professional mastery although they could and did root Australian writing in its native soil. So successful were they in this task that it is fairly commonplace to find Australian poets and critics today attacking the tyranny of the bush tradition. "One cannot help feeling that Australian poets," writes one of them, A. D. Hope, "treat their country very much as the Australian land-grabbers did: they have exploited it for all it was worth; and after the grand rake-off of the vulgarian nineties, one observes that the end of the process has been much the same in both cases: impoverishment and erosion. In spite of improved techniques, the returns grow steadily less, the effects thinner. The impression of reading the annual anthologies is that of poetry slowly hardening into a single vast geographical cliche." [31] "The poets," writes another of them, Vincent Buckley, "are dazed by the size of the land. . . . They ought, rather, to be amazed by her destiny and should seek to make their poetry a way of comprehending and recreating it." [32]

The remedy is in their own hands. The society they now live in is a different one from that which bred the first generation of bush writers, and if they are up to its challenge, it will not clip their wings overmuch. Meanwhile, needing no longer to be aggressively Australian, they have been picking up once more the threads of the European tradition to which they belong.

Not that this tradition had been fully cast aside, even by the bush writers, but they had been amateurs, not fully masters of its technical achievement. The two Australian writers of that time of undoubted stature happen to be the two whose work was rooted in European tradition and whose approach to their craft was professional. Christopher Brennan and Henry Handel

31. "Australian Poetry—A Geographical Cliché?" *Voice*, V (1956), 12.

32. "A New Bulletin School?" *The Port Phillip Gazette* (Melbourne), II (1954), 20.

Richardson were born in the same year, 1870, the poet in Sydney, the novelist in Melbourne. Their differing fates may illustrate the difficulties of achieving a professional culture in the utilitarian, friendly, uncritical colonial society into which they were born. Ethel Richardson, who wrote her novels under the name of Henry Handel Richardson, left Melbourne for Leipzig at the age of seventeen to study music, returning only for a visit in 1912 to gather material for her trilogy, *The Fortunes of Richard Mahoney* (1917–1929). Although almost all her writing was spun from her girlhood in Australia, her career resembles that of Alexander the philosopher, in that it required migration to an overseas environment more favourable to work of professional quality. Believing that her talents were not those required for the best work in music, she abandoned the professional study of it in favour of writing, pursuing perfection in that art with an austerity which contrasts with the easygoing flabbiness, the mere approximation in the expression of ideas, that marked most colonial writing. The necessity of such austere devotion was the essential theme of her first novel, *Maurice Guest* (1908). Her trilogy, *The Fortunes of Richard Mahoney*, draws its tragic theme from her Australian experience and presents its Australian material with unerring authenticity; but it is a great novel in the European mainstream of the nineteenth century. It could have been written only by an Australian, but it could scarcely have been written at that time by an Australian who had no other experience, for it is doubtful whether Australia could have taught the young girl who left it in 1887 the austere discipline that such a work required, the discipline to which she was first introduced by her study of music in Leipzig.

Christopher Brennan's career re-enforces this argument, although he wrote his poems in Australia. Sydney University gave the young student of obvious scholastic promise a grounding in classics and philosophy and a travelling scholarship to the University of Berlin. There in 1892 and 1893 he read widely in the classics and in English, French, German, and Italian literature, and acquired his abiding interest in French symbolist poetry. His first scholarly article, "On the Manuscripts of Aeschylus," was published in *The Journal of Philology* in 1893. He returned to Australia, working as a librarian and as a part-time university teacher. The opportunities for a scholarly livelihood were still too few to enable him to return to a position which would have favoured an uninterrupted development of his scholarly or poetic promise. He was later to become Professor of German in the University of Sydney and it was my own good fortune to attend that university early enough to hear him, not on German literature but on Homer, in his last year as a university professor.

Brennan's great powers were to peter out at length in an alcoholic futility, and both his scholarly and his poetic output were small. It is beyond my scope and my intention to pursue the tragedy of this most powerful of Australian poets into those of its sources which were personal and domestic. The long delay in finding a university appointment may well have blurred his scholarly hopes. The University gave him some colleagues who could call his imagination to life, and above all, J. LeGay Brereton, the Elizabethan scholar and his great friend, who was my professor of English literature in Sydney. But Sydney could not then offer the sustained and crowded intellectual stimulus that he might have found in Europe. Furthermore, the universities of that time, regarded rather as institutions for training teachers, lawyers, and doctors than as centres of learning, demanded too wide a scatter of effort from their still small number of teachers. Having in my own time seen a transformation which now allows a university scholar in Australia to concentrate his efforts, I know well how easily the versatility demanded by those earlier conditions destroyed many a scholarly ambition. For I return to the point that work of the highest order in scholarship, literature or the arts requires a full-time and life-long concentration of effort in the mastery of one's craft. The late colonial society of Australia in 1900 gave neither a full stimulus to such a life nor many opportunities to lead it. This may not explain the tragic waste of Brennan's life, but it certainly helps to explain the thinness of his output, both in scholarship and in poetry.

But there is another thing. A scholar and poet who was sensitively responsive to the spirit of his time and place, Brennan found little nourishment in its shallow fare. He shared the idealistic impulses of his generation, and the poems of his *The Burden of Tyre*,[33] a sequence written for the most part between September, 1900, and May, 1901, express the horror he had brought back from his years in Germany of the destructive militarism which he saw threatening the world once more at the time of the Boer War. In the face of that awakening evil, the comfortable assurance of his own people, as of those like them elsewhere in the world, appalled him, and he saw the flabbiness of a vague idealism which substituted mere doing for the horrors of thought. A still colonial society, not yet ready in 1900 for men of his stature, had nourished little writing in a man whose greatness of mind might have flowered in Europe; but perhaps it was the very quality of that colonial society with its proud material achievements and its thin life of the spirit which inspired the work which most displayed his power, *The Wanderer*. As you listen to these few lines from one of the *Wanderer* poems, you will know at once that here was work of no colonial mediocrity:

I cry to you as I pass your windows in the dusk;
Ye have built you unmysterious homes and ways in the wood
where of old ye went with sudden eyes to the right and left;
and your going was now made safe, and your staying comforted,
for the fresh edge itself, holding old savagery
in unsearch'd glooms, was your house's friendly barrier.
And now that the year goes winterward, ye thought to hide
behind your gleaming panes, and where the hearth sings merrily
make cheer with meat and wine, and sleep in the long night,
and the uncared wastes might be a crying unhappiness.
But I, who have come from the outer night, I say to you

33. Published posthumously in 1954.

the winds are up and terribly will they shake the dry wood:
the woods shall awake, hearing them, shall awake to be toss'd and
 riven,
and make a cry and a parting in your sleep all night
as the wither'd leaves go whirling all night along all ways.
And when ye come forth at dawn, uncomforted by sleep,
ye shall stand at amaze, beholding all the ways overhidden
with worthless drift of the dead and all your broken world:
and ye shall not know whence the winds have come, nor shall ye
 know
whither the yesterdays have fled, or if they were.[34]

In this lecture I have explored, all too incompletely, some
of the conditions which bear on the birth and growth of culture
in new lands; for such lands, if they must draw on their in-
heritance, cannot merely take over a culture ready-made. A
native Australian literature and a native art were born in the
period we have examined, but maturity had to await conditions not then present in adequate measure. It required a
widening and deepening of experience in a community no
longer sheltered, by a power not its own, from the perils of the
world. It also required something more tangible, an increase
in the scale of the resources devoted to intellectual and artistic
activity. The former requirement has surely been met by our
exposure to the dangerous world of this century. The latter
requirement is partly a function of expanding size and wealth,
but also of a changing valuation of the things of the mind. In
my third and final lecture I shall explore the identity and difference of a nation which has been transformed in numbers
and occupations during the last half-century but which still
clings to its older traditions. That nation has now entered, I
believe on the evidence, a phase of its history which exposes
it to great dangers but allows an achievement, limited, no
doubt, in scale, but of a depth and richness unknown in its past
history.

34. In George Mackaness, ed., *An Anthology of Australian Verse*
(Sydney: Angus and Robertson, 1952), p. 33.

III

"Coming of Age"

In these three lectures, I have had it in mind to present one Australian's thoughts about the history and character of his country. The degree to which these thoughts may rest on faith and untestable speculation has been concealed by the historical and documented nature of the material so far used. As we approach the present, the element of faith must come into the open. For I believe that Australia, a small nation living on the fringes of an island-continent which is as large as the United States excluding Alaska but which contains barely ten million people, may now be on the verge of an achievement matching the dangers and the difficulties to which it is exposed.

Clarity of vision has been a rare thing in the world's history, and those who have possessed it, whether Athenians or Florentines, have been found uncomfortable neighbours by those whose vision has been more decently veiled. At his best—and I base this belief on a quarter-century's close study of the habits of mind of the best Australian students—the Australian appears to me to be acquiring a habit of looking at things straight and clear which may grow into that type of vision. It requires further schooling yet, in the more complex, more subtle experience of the wider world to which he is now so fully exposed. But it would be a mistake to suppose him barred by the smallness of his numbers from distinction in the activities of mind any more than he has been barred by that same smallness of numbers from distinction in those other things to which he has turned his attention—together with the determination

51

and endurance of which he is occasionally capable—the cricket field, the tennis court, and the mile track.

I began the first of these lectures by stating my belief that the dead-level interpretation of Australian history was misleading. That interpretation, although seemingly supported by the democratic cast of Australian institutions and by a relatively mediocre achievement in the life of the spirit, appeared to be based on two misconceptions, that Australian history was unrelievedly democratic, and that democracy was necessarily hostile to distinction. Against the former assumption stands the strongly aristocratic pattern of much of Australian social history. Against the latter stands the observation that a thinness in the life of the spirit has been a common quality of a colonial and passing *phase* of development on which lasting predictions cannot be based.

The thinness or mediocrity of the late colonial culture of Australia was emphasised by its assertive revolt against social and literary conventions, the chief protagonists of which had been too imitative of the old world and somewhat too patronizing of the new and cruder world growing up about them to create an indigenous and growing culture. Influenced overmuch by the loud denunciations of the *Bulletin*, historians have too easily neglected the genuine cultivation of the more conservative and respectable sections of society. Those whose habit it was to read the close-printed editorials of *The Argus*, who attended the meetings of the Shakespearian Society or of the Royal Society, and who subscribed to the more serious journals of Edinburgh and London were neither ignorant nor merely provincial. But in so far as the leaders of education and polite letters were taken to be conservative and English, assertion of independence took on a radical and aggressively Australian tone. "Temper democratic: bias offensively Australian" was Joseph Furphy's own description of his novel, *Such is Life*. But the intellectual and artistic limitations of the achievements of this phase of revolt was a quality less of its politics than of the relatively unsophisticated stage of colonial development at that time. It was a society which proved able to nourish the beginnings of some great talents, such as those of Samuel Alexander, Henry Handel Richardson, and Christopher Brennan; but it could not then bring such talents to fruition. Australians have taken a just pride in the high achievement of some of their fellows in the scholarly, professional, and artistic circles of the old world, but it has been a mark of immaturity that our more brilliant youngsters have been faced with a choice between achievement in exile and frustration at home. The measure of increasing maturity is the increasing proportion who now find sufficient opportunity in their native land.

Immaturity in the life of the spirit was only to be expected, then, so long as colonial society continued to be sheltered by British power from the challenges of the world at large, so long as it continued to be preoccupied with those tasks of pioneering which bred admiration of action rather than of reflection, and so long as it offered relatively meagre opportunities for a professional life in scholarship, literature, and the arts. In reverse, the conditions of a more mature life of the spirit are to be sought: first, in increasing and deepening experience of an intractable world; second, in the growth of the society in the variety of its occupations, the complexity of its required skills and the consequent sophistication of an increasing proportion of its people; and finally, and perhaps as a consequence of these things, in the diversion of a larger proportion of its wealth to the things of the spirit.

Whether the democratic cast achieved by Australian society in this century has indeed proved, as is often said, unsympathetic to the full encouragement of these last remains an open question; but it is at least clear that the spiritual limitations of colonial society in 1900 did not provide an answer to that question one way or the other, since they might prove temporary. It is too often supposed that the judgment is clear, that the democratic temper, confirmed by the changes of this century, continues to prefer the middling standard and to be either hostile to distinction or merely indifferent to it. But if democracy does in truth present difficulties because its leaders have to be persuaded to support adventures of the mind which may be outside their range of understanding, it may nevertheless be a necessary condition of that type of direct vision which I believe to be growing in the best Australians. For clarity of vision is not easily bred in a society governed by an instinctive cringe towards the respectable classes.

Whatever may be said of these difficult matters, it must be admitted that Australia's increased exposure to the world seemed for a long time in this century to nourish anything but clarity of mind.

It is true that the clouding of faith and vision was a little delayed; for in the first decade of the new Commonwealth, the liberals, led by Deakin and supported by the new Labour Party, continued with the optimism of glad morning the task of building a just society. One of the chief architects of the new Commonwealth, Attorney-General in its first Government, and Prime Minister on three occasions between 1903 and 1910, Alfred Deakin did more than any other person to shape the infant Commonwealth in those first and most formative years. His Government depended for three of them on the support of the Labour Party, and it was to prove an easy mode of attack later for Labour politicians to claim that they had called the tune to which he had merely danced. But the Deakin papers confirm the impression of his public statements that the programme of social welfare which he carried out was rooted in his own deepest convictions. Religious without attachment to dogma, liberal without surrender to doctrine, Deakin was impressed in fact and not merely in word by the responsibility which rested on him and his fellows, the first makers of the new Commonwealth, to imprint on it as its first pattern the stamp of justice resting on law. The bank crash and the depression of the 1890's, when not only the speculative land and building companies tumbled but even thirteen of Australia's twenty-five banks suspended payments, Deakin had seen as a punishment visited on the colonists for the blind and selfish vice of money-grabbing which took no care of one's neighbour but sought only the enrichment of oneself, that speculation which had reigned uncontrolled, optimistic and blind in the "marvellous Melbourne" of the boom years. Among the Deakin papers are many manuscript prayers, written in the privacy of his study in those early hours of the morning which were his time for private reading and reflection. These prayers are full of the agonised recognition that he also had sinned, in his satisfaction with the evident material progress of his time, in common with those whose financial gambles had tumbled into the wreckage of the nineties. His unstinted labours for federation were in some sense a constructive penance, but only if the federation were such that it matched its progress with its justice.

Moreover, the industrial strife of "the Great Strikes" which had hung over water-front and shearing sheds from 1889 to 1894—in those same troubled years of bank crashes and depression—had impressed Deakin and other liberals of his stamp with a horror of the rising threat of class war and a determination to prevent it. By curbing the harshness of a competitive society, they hoped to remove the bitterness which served as incentive to class war, and by offering an alternative procedure in the method of conciliation and arbitration in a court of law they hoped to make class war an anachronism.

The programme which Deakin carried out as Prime Minister was not, then, a mere concession to Labour's prodding, but an attempt to translate into practical legislation a set of ideals deeply held. There was no lack in the Commonwealth Parliament of that competition for place, prominence, and profit which constitutes so much of politics; but Deakin stood above it, despite the natural enjoyment of a gifted politician in political manoeuvre, and there were enough like him to form a genuinely liberal party.

But if Deakin's programme was his own and no mere labour graft on the liberal stem, it is also true that in those earlier happier days than those about to dawn, there was no sense of a gulf fixed, but only a difference of degree between liberals and labour men who had also rejected the methods of class war. The early labour leaders in the Commonwealth Parliament, J. C. Watson, Andrew Fisher, even the fiery little Welshman, William Morris Hughes, seemed liberals like themselves. It is true that they were distinguished by a readiness to carry state intervention a little further and to sacrifice private judgment to party solidarity in a manner then unacceptable to liberals. But the Deakin who had long ago fought with determination in the Victorian Parliament to control the rising evil of sweated labour could not in principle disagree with Hughes when he defined the Labour view of the use of the state: "We say that the strong arm of the State should interfere between the socially strong and the socially weak. We say that the State should interfere with the man who by birth or chance of fortune had become possessed of the means of production by which alone we can earn our living, so that he shall not crush his fellow-men, so that he shall no longer have the right to say under what conditions and how long his fellow-creatures shall work." [1]

How far that "strong arm of the State" should be used was a matter of debate and of changing adjustment to needs and opinions from time to time, as indeed it has continued to be ever since in Australia as in other Western democracies. Labour would use it with less fear that the helpful state might grow into a devouring Leviathan, and indeed some toughness and obstinancy of temper bred in them by their experience in dealing with the trade unions further marked them off. But such

1. Cited by W. Farmer Whyte, *William Morris Hughes: His Life and Times* (Sydney: Angus and Robertson, 1957), p. 69.

differences were in abeyance in the days of the liberal-labour alliance. This alliance established the policy called "the new protection" which was perhaps best expressed by Mr. Justice Higgins in a famous judgment in the Commonwealth Court of Conciliation and Arbitration. For if the very establishment of that court had expressed the belief that industrial relations could be made "a new province for law and order," Higgins' declaration of a basic wage drew out the implicit assumption that the laws of economic competition might be controlled by a principle of justice. In an article called "A New Province for Law and Order" which he wrote for the *Harvard Law Review* in 1915, Higgins avowed the further faith that made all the particular reforms seem but steps towards a richer life:

In conclusion, I may state that I am not unaware of the far-reaching schemes, much discussed everywhere, which contemplate conditions of society in which the adjustment of labour conditions between profit-makers and wage-earners may become unnecessary. Our Australian Court has nothing to do with these schemes. It has to shape its conclusions on the solid anvil of existing industrial facts, in the fulfilment of definite official responsibilities. . . . Yet though the functions of the Court are definite and limited, there is opened up for idealists a very wide horizon; . . . men . . . are willing to work, but even good work does not necessarily insure a proper human subsistence, and when they protest against this condition of things they are told that their aims are too "materialistic." Give them relief from their materialistic anxiety; give them reasonable certainty that their essential material needs will be met by honest work, and you release infinite stores of human energy for higher efforts, for nobler ideals, when
> "Body gets sop, and holds its noise, and
> leaves soul free a little."

Even if it is agreed that the Court did stabilise wage movements and maintain peace in its own sectors of Australian industry to 1916, these results may seem a diluted answer to such high hopes; but at least the liberals of the early Commonwealth did have a programme which was not mere opportunism.

"The positive content of Deakin's programme," says Professor Greenwood,

reflects points by point the more mature aspects of Australian nationalism. Protection to manufacturers against outside competition is balanced by "new protection" which seeks to spread the rewards to labour as well as to capital. State mediation is the sword to slay the ogre of class war, and arbitration and the basic wage are the means to ensure that the rule of law shall guarantee fair dealing and minimum economic justice. Social services recognize the contributions made by the aged in their working years and the obligations of society to the invalid and the needy. Defence preparations, notably the design of an Australian navy as well as the expression of Australian views on Pacific issues, bespeak the development of an independent mentality and a willingness to shoulder increased responsibility.[2]

The measured progress of those years was carried on from 1910 to 1913 with little obvious change of intention or of pace by the Labour Government of Andrew Fisher. And yet the manner in which the alliance of Deakin's liberals with labour had been replaced by opposition between them had cast some doubt on the assumption of a harmony of interests in a society of expanding justice. For Australian liberals shared the dilemma besetting all liberals who had accepted the view that the power of the state could justly be used to control the anarchy of competition. Having accepted the intervention of the state on behalf of justice, they could not point to any logical stopping point; but they could and did feel a growing alarm at the evident readiness of some labour members to go much further along the road of state action than they. Having ousted Deakin and established a labour government at the end of 1908, labour members bitterly attacked Deakin for forming in reply a fusion-party with his old opponents on the conservative side of the house. "... I heard from this side of the house," said Hughes, "some mention of Judas. I do not agree with that:

2. Gordon Greenwood, *Australia: A Social and Political History* (Sydney: Angus and Robertson, 1955), p. 216.

it is not fair—to Judas, for whom there is this to be said, that he did not gag the man whom he betrayed, nor did he fail to hang himself afterwards." [3] For Deakin no attack could equal his own anguish at finding himself, as it seemed, leading a party of his old enemies in opposition to a party of progress. And yet what seemed to be a loss of direction was in fact a necessary and inevitable growth of the two-party system, the absence of which Deakin had himself so often deplored; and it was not that decline into class war crystallised in party that so many, liberals and conservatives alike, feared.

Yet the easy days of harmonious advance along the road of social justice were ending. The world was sick, and not even the remote Antipodes could escape its contagion. The increase of rivalry between the armed camps of Europe was matched across the world by a toughening of temper in industrial relations as Capital and Labour looked at each other across an abyss deepened by fanatic doctrine. In Australia, Mr. Justice Higgins' Commonwealth Court managed, mainly by concessions, to maintain harmony in those sectors of industry which it could control, but the state tribunals were less fortunate. From 1908 to 1914, in New South Wales and Queensland in particular, industrial strife deepened in a time of rising prices and uncertain employment. In 1913, when 35 per cent of Australian Unionists belonged to unions numbering more than ten thousand members, the large aggregations of workmen which already existed in the railways and tramways, on the wharves, coal-fields, and lead-mines, and in the new blast-furnaces, were, in such conditions, responsive to the syndicalist propaganda of the Industrial Workers of the World, and at least more prone to turn away from parliamentary to direct action, to the method of the strike.

With the outbreak of world war in 1914, the rising discord was concealed by patriotic emotions, but only for a time. In 1915, pride in the exploits of the Anzacs at Gallipoli was ac-

3. *Commonwealth Parliamentary Debates*, Vol. 49, p. 175.

companied by heavy hearts as the first, long, casualty lists were published; and the more frothy emotions of 1914 were replaced in the thoughtful by a deeper understanding of the costs of those responsibilities which Australians had demanded as their right in the Imperial Conferences of 1907 and 1911. Easter, 1916, brought the Sinn Fein Rebellion to divide the loyalties of those Australians, almost a quarter of the total, who were of Irish descent or birth. In the same year the prime minister, William Morris Hughes, returned from Europe convinced that the system of voluntary enlistment must be replaced by conscription if the Australian forces overseas were to be maintained at full strength. Unable to carry his own party with him, the Labour Prime Minister twice appealed to the people by referendum. Australians, who enlisted 416,809 volunteers in a population which did not reach 5,000,000 until 1918, rejected this proposal on both occasions, after a controversy which divided them more bitterly and more deeply, I believe, than they had ever been divided before. For conscription became an issue in which all the strong passions of the time, relevant and irrelevant, were expressed. Resentment of Ireland's wrongs was countered bitterly by denunciation of what was regarded as Irish treachery, and one Irish Australian's attack in 1920 on what he called "this bloody and accursed empire" [4] did nothing to still the unabated storm. Industrial strife, checked in 1914, broke out with a multiplied fury in 1916 and 1917, and who could estimate the respective shares in responsibility for those strikes of the I.W.W., rising costs, and unstable employment? As troubles rose, the arbitrariness of the government increased, inexperienced as it was in the necessary censorship of war-time and led by its ebullient prime minister in carelessness of those traditional rights of free speech which threatened him with opposition.

4. Hugh Mahon (1858–1931). Because of this remark, Mahon was expelled from the Federal House of Representatives.—*Commonwealth Parliamentary Debates,* Vol. 94, p. 6383.

The conscription campaigns did untold damage to an old liberal tradition. The labour parties of states and commonwealth, split irreparably by their hostilities on this issue, lost their leaders to their opponents, and, defeated in all but one state, took on the more doctrinaire colour of mere parties of opposition, while the old liberalism of their lost leaders foundered in the storms of war, industrial strife, and faction.

Nor did the peace, so deeply longed for, heal these wounds. Industrial troubles reached their height in 1919, when, with political labour in opposition, the unions turned more easily to direct action and accepted more readily the leadership of minorities influenced by the Bolshevik Revolution. As usual, Frank Wilmot, the Melbourne poet, caught the temper of the time; Frank Wilmot whose poems with their quiet passion and acute perception, serve as a Greek chorus to show us the meaning of those events:

> The fumes of the ancient hells have invaded your spirit,
> And old reputed disaster has broken your heart. . . .
>
> Brooding on the Romanoffs, the Syndicates, the Boyne!
> Shuddering in echoes of ceaseless war and causeless revolution,
> Drowned in echoes of reflected troubles.
> Dying amid your groves of golden trees,
> Surrounded by the unregarded dawn! [5]

In the mean decade of the 1920's when, in Australia as elsewhere, an unsettled generation sought in excitements some alternatives to the sense of direction and purpose which it lacked, the doctrinal dramatics of these struggles faded out to the radical fringes of industrial and political labour, and Australian political life returned to the humdrum normality of piecemeal bargaining. But neither in politics nor in economics was it a return to full health.

The old belief in liberal progress was not recovered and indeed one is conscious of loss of leadership. I have long believed

5. "Echoes," in *Poems by Furnley Maurice (Frank Wilmot)*, selected by Percival Serle (Melbourne: Lothian Publishing Co., 1944).

that there was a particular reason for this which is often over-
looked. Australia had enlisted over 400,000 soldiers and sent
329,000 of them overseas, a large number for a small population of under five million people. In the later years of the war
they were used on the Western Front as shock troops and their
casualties were heavy, totalling 323,000. Of these, close on
60,000 were killed in battle or died of wounds. All this, while
a source of melancholy pride and a tribute to the courage and
fighting dash of the men who fought, is a standing condemna-
tion of those who so ill-used these splendid but scarce resources, and it has to be put to the credit of William Morris
Hughes that he presented Haig with an ultimatum to have
them rested at last. Sixty thousand may seem a small number
beside the millions killed in that war of the trenches, but it
was not a small proportion of the young men of Australia, and
there is some reason to believe that it included a high proportion of those young men of promise who might have been expected to supply the new generation with its leaders. This remains to be investigated, but I am conscious in my own retrospect of a hiatus: in those years after the war when I was a
schoolboy and an undergraduate, I can think of only one of
my teachers of note who belonged to that generation of soldiers. We were taught by the middle-aged and the aged, and
we too much lacked the bridge between of those nearer our
own age who might have guided us safely past some of the
pits into which we fell. How many were there like Mervyn
Higgins, the son of Henry Bourne Higgins, the predestined
leaders, who did not return?

The feverish business activity of the 1920's did not conceal
from a clear-sighted group of economists the dangers besetting
an economy which nourished uneconomic industries behind
ever-rising tariff walls, spent millions of pounds on unsuccessful
attempts to settle returned soldiers and immigrants on the
land, and surrendered to every sectional demand for subsidy.

The Great Depression of the 1930's had other causes than

these internal weaknesses; but it made them clear to all, and with them, the backwardness in social legislation of a country which had so long rested on its much vaunted laurels of an earlier age of reform. Only Queensland possessed a public system of unemployment relief when the impact of depression raised even registered unemployment to 29 per cent. If, as I have remarked elsewhere,[6] adversity calls out greatness, Australians in common with many other peoples of the world were then in the way of it; but in fact it meant for many the frustration of old hopes, and a ready response to the alternative promises of doctrinaire ideologies. Meanwhile, "doles and relief work miserably dragged out the time; and many unaccustomed feet trod the streets and the bush roads wearily and unsuccessfully seeking work,"[7] or trying to sell unsaleable goods to those who had no money to buy them. It was Frank Wilmot again who most truly captured the feeling of that time, Frank Wilmot, so kind and gentle in person, so romantic in imagination, but so determined not to allow sentimental fancy to conceal clear sight:

> But I'm not weaving sentimental stories
> About these boots and their departed glories,

he wrote in his poem "Upon a Row of Old Boots and Shoes in a Pawnbroker's Window";

> Up to blue heaven my entreaty rises
> For food, for shelter, and not to pawn my shoes.

The depression ended the superficial optimism of the twenties and brought more people to listen to the economists and geographers who expounded the economic and physical necessities of Australian life. But it also brought in its train an increase in the influence of the doctrinaire in the industrial and political life of the country. There were obvious reasons for this beyond the search for remedy for such disastrous ills. The

6. *Australia* (London: Hutchinson's University Library, 1952), p. 174.
7. *Ibid.*

increasing scale both of industrial enterprises and of the trade unions had made industrial relations more impersonal, more easily viewed as a war of Capital and Labour. That tendency had been confirmed in many labour men by the Commonwealth Bank's obstruction of labour policy during the depression, and by the evident tenderness which non-labour governments continued to show to private enterprise in destroying, in its favour, a number of state enterprises, including a number of reasonably successful state enterprises, which had been established by labour governments.

The rise of totalitarian régimes in Europe and Japan, and the successive and successful aggressions committed by them during the 1930's kept ideological discussion alive and bitter. The noise of controversy, however, can be misleading, and in the event it was to appear that an old readiness to solve heated controversy by practical compromise was still strong; but certainly in those years it was often difficult to read the facts aright, so many were the distorting mirrors held to them.

The second world war brought greater dangers than ever before in its history to a country which had shown signs in the late 1930's of discovering its way once more. Pearl Harbor found Australia virtually defenceless, all her trained forces overseas. Mr. Curtin, the new labour Prime Minister, overruled Mr. Churchill and insisted that the Australian divisions should return to Australia's defence, and in a speech which recognized facts but aroused great criticism declared: "Without any inhibitions of any kind, I make it quite clear that Australia looks to America, free of any pangs as to our traditional links of kinship with the United Kingdom. We know the problems that the United Kingdom faces. We know the constant threat of invasion. We know the dangers of dispersal of strength. But we know, too, that Australia can go and Britain still hold on. We are therefore determined that Australia shall not go, and we shall exert all our energies towards the shaping of a plan, with the United States as its keystone, which will give to our country some confidence of being able to hold out until the tide of battle swings against the enemy." [8]

How superbly Mr. Curtin's appeal to America was answered, the battles of the Coral Sea and Midway, and the long fight back to Japan, may attest; and that Australians, in that time of danger when divisions dropped away and they became a community, were ready to support that appeal by self-help may also be attested by the enrolment of almost one million of their seven million people in the armed services.

In the first world war, a labour government had been split by dispute on the conscription question: in the depression, another labour government was destroyed by dispute over remedies: but the second world war saw a third labour government rise to the challenge of the times and grow in stature and confidence as it led the country in war and prepared for a juster peace. That this was more than a particular and accidental growth in one political party is shown by the fact that the new certainty of touch and imagination in government which marked this time were continued when that government was replaced by its opponents in 1949.

It was in this period of war that Australian public life moved clearly out of a tentative apprenticeship into a professional efficiency. This owed much to the readiness of the Labour Party to use industrialists who were its traditional opponents and academics whom it traditionally distrusted, in administering its war effort and in drafting its plans both for war and peace.

Australian observers have recognized the forced growth of the war years, when Australia was for the first time faced with a real and not as in the past with an imaginary danger of invasion. "For many years," writes Professor Partridge, "it has been a cliché of Australian oratory that Australia achieved nationhood through the exploits of her troops at Gallipoli in 1915. It could be argued that the second world-war brought

8. Cited in Greenwood, *Australia*, p. 397.

about a much more decisive advance towards national maturity. . . . Nor can there be any doubt that the dramatic demonstration of national capacity, political, economic, military and diplomatic that was given between 1941 and 1945 quickened the pulse of national life. Of course it is a common thing for war, desperately but successfully fought, to produce a general sense of new and greater potentialities; whether the feeling of exhilaration will continue to animate public life after the end of the struggle is another matter. In the case of Australia," concludes Professor Partridge, "it is difficult to say whether the imaginativeness and the drive developed during the years of war have continued to make themselves felt in national affairs since it ended." [9]

If I feel at least a tempered optimism about the answer to this question, it is for two sorts of reasons. The more obvious is the extent and the continuing nature of the achievement; the less obvious is its pre-war source, its being rooted, that is to say, in something less ephemeral than the temporary stimulus of danger. The achievement has indeed been impressive and its relative expertness and flexibility stand in marked contrast with the blundering attempts at post-war settlement after the first world war. It is beyond the possibilities of an hour's lecture to examine the later achievement, beyond pointing to its major divisions. In a reasonably expert fashion the community evolved policies of social welfare and full employment which have proved sound. Firmly rejecting the antipathy of the 1930's towards immigration in general and Southern European immigration in particular, it has introduced, by means of a vigorous and imaginative immigration policy, over one million persons into the country since the war. It has embarked on vigorous development of resources to enable these numbers to be absorbed. It has adopted, if a little slowly, policies to control inflation which have required measures such as high taxation demanding unusual political courage. Further, if the achieve-

9. In Greenwood, *Australia,* pp. 405–6.

ment still falls short of what some of us desire, the community has diverted a much larger proportion of its wealth to the education of its people, the pursuit of new knowledge, and even to the cultivation of the arts, than at any time past.

In their external relations, both of trade and diplomacy, Australian governments have developed, after some exaggerations, an independent initiative and a professional flexibility of policy, limited inevitably by the rigidities of the cold war and the smallness of Australian power and resources. In the backward territories of Papua and New Guinea, Australians are responsible for the welfare of one and three-quarter millions of native peoples who "speak between 200 and 300 different languages," some of them living "in villages perched on remote mountain ridges; some ... deep in the jungle; some in large coastal villages; some on or about the many waterways of the Fly and Sepik rivers; some in the hundreds of outlying islands" —people who range from primitive savages to those who, as the present Minister responsible for their welfare has put it, "own and conduct their own enterprises ... enjoy cash incomes and have bank balances,—own motor vehicles and ... run their own affairs and take an active part in village affairs through their local Government Councils. ... Men who were subject to the fear of the sorcerer," continues Mr. Hasluck, "and who had never travelled beyond their own valleys five years ago are today having their diseases cured with anti-biotics, and men who spent a lusty youth in murderous warfare with their neighbours are now being asked to forget the cannibal feast and all become politicians in their middle age." [10] It would be a fascinating subject to pursue the attempts to guide these people into well-being and self-government. I must be content with this one comment that I have yet to meet the educated Australian who has visited these territories, perhaps pre-

10. Paul M. C. Hasluck, "Australia's Task in Papua and New Guinea," 7th Roy Milne Memorial Lecture, Australian Institute of International Affairs, Melbourne, 1956, pp. 20, 25.

disposed to criticism, who has not returned deeply impressed by the flexibility of policy and by the calibre of those, whether in health, education, or government, who are concerned with its translation into action.

These positive tasks were necessarily accompanied by the negative task of defending the established order against subversion. The stresses of post-war reconstruction provided troubled waters for communists to fish in and they did not neglect their opportunities. But if their activities threatened the successful conduct of our constructive tasks, there was also the danger that Australian democracy might be subverted by the very methods used to protect it. Australia was fortunate in that it did on the whole escape a dangerous hysteria in the face of undoubted communist provocation. The Communist Party Dissolution Bill introduced by the Liberal and Country Party Government of Mr. Menzies was declared invalid by the High Court in March, 1951, while power to enact such legislation was refused by a narrow margin in a referendum later in the same year. Many at least of those who voted "no" did so because of a distrust of legislation which they believed threatened to destroy the liberal tradition of the country. Only those who had a vested interest in rigged elections, however, have regretted the more constructive measures which obliged trade unions to elect their officials by supervised secret ballot. The decline of communist influence in the unions coincides with this measure.

The record is indeed impressive both on the positive side of constructive achievement and on the negative side of the avoidance of hysteria. But so mature an achievement could not have emerged merely out of the sudden stimulus of war, and, indeed a closer view discloses clear signs of a new level of maturity and professional skill in Australian life in those years before the war, the late 1930's when Australia was emerging from the depression. It is true that the passions stirred by the world's march into disaster in those years somewhat obscured this truth; but the evidence crowds in on the historian as he looks for the signs of growing maturity that a corner was turned in Australian history at that time. Rarely indeed is one given the means of dating the coming of age of a new nation so precisely as they are given in this case.

It was at this time that the Commonwealth Public Service began to enlist a proportion of university graduates for general administration. Outside certain departments such as the Attorney-General's, which required professional qualifications, the Public Service had too often been the comfortable home of mediocrities recruited at a low scholastic level and safely defended from those with imagination by a seniority rule in promotion. It is true that the recruitment of first-class graduates was slow to mount as they turned to careers less blasted by a reputation for rewarding mediocrity; but it is also true that this period did see the recruitment of some men of outstanding quality. War-time recruitment of academics added to their number.

The same picture of a lift in the level of Australian life is found to be true outside government as well as in it. It was in 1937, for instance, that the Council for Scientific and Industrial Research, founded in 1926, was enlarged to carry out research relevant to secondary industry as well as that in the problems of the pastoral and agricultural industries which had previously been its concern. The needs of war hastened a development already evident before war broke out, and the Commonwealth Scientific and Industrial Research Organisation as it is now known has come to vie with the universities in pure as well as in applied science. The universities themselves were stirring in those years just before the war. In the University of Sydney, a conservative dullness which had come to mark it in my undergraduate days despite the continuing presence of some great men, was being swept away by a number of new brooms. In Melbourne, a great era of experimental reform, not yet spent, was initiated by the appointment of Dr. Raymond Priestley as Vice-Chancellor in 1935. Their internal quickening gave rise, inevitably, to a more active intervention in public affairs, an intervention not always welcomed by those persons in the community who believed that universities should be content to produce lawyers, doctors, engineers, and teachers of perfect orthodoxy. Neither such reactions nor the dependence of Australian universities on governments for money have curtailed their freedom, and indeed it was precisely at this time of the increasing participation of the university teachers in public controversies that the state governments began to lift the level of their grants.

In the arts as well as in government and scholarship, there was also an evident quickening in those years. The Australian Broadcasting Commission, established in 1932, began its education of Australians in good music on a nation-wide scale that had been impossible for the meagrely supported Conservatorium Orchestras of Sydney, Melbourne, and Adelaide. Musical composition is the last, as it is the most highly sophisticated, of the arts to appear in a new country, but at least its beginnings were evident at this time. In literature, if no major work appeared in those years, at least the city began to claim the attention of novelists and poetry to take on a less amateurish quality. In architecture, most building continued to be undistinguished, but Roy Grounds, an architect of genius in Melbourne, was already producing the ideas that others were in time to turn into architectural clichés.

The demands of war and the stimulus given to further effort by the discovery of unsuspected capacities immensely increased the scale of all these activities. Indeed, looking back over the last twenty years, one is most aware of the change of scale. Beginning from so far back, the scale may still seem small; but one is conscious that in the last twenty years, and above all in the last ten, and in a wide variety of fields both of action and of thought, we have emerged from the stage of frustrating impossibility into that in which it may still be difficult but is no longer impossible to do work of really professional quality.

And if, within these various fields of thought and action, one emphasises the changed scale of financial provision for those activities which are of the mind and imagination, this is not to suppose that adequate material provision is sufficient in itself to ensure the finest achievements in these realms. But if livelihood is not a sufficient condition, it is at least a necessary condition, and one of the most striking signs of the newly achieved sophistication of Australian society has been the readiness of those who hold its purse-strings to divert to the life of the mind a suddenly increased proportion of its resources. In many fields, the scale is inadequate still; but it is also true that in many of them it is now possible for the first time in Australia to do professional work. It would be tedious to put before you the figures showing the changed scale of commonwealth and state assistance to scientific research, for example, or to the universities more generally. One example, near to my experience, must convey the broader implication. In 1939, there were, I think, twelve of us teaching history full-time in six Australian universities in which, for all subjects, perhaps twelve thousand students were enrolled; this year (1958), there are approximately one hundred full-time historians on the staff of nine universities in which close on forty thousand students are enrolled. For the first time it has become possible for the Australian university historian to restrict the scatter of his activities within reasonable limits and to do first-class work within them. And as the opportunities grow, so we are retaining more of our most gifted people or attracting them back to us. The export of brilliant youngsters was a mark of our intellectual immaturity; the retention in Australia of such men as our third holder of the Order of Merit, Sir Macfarlane Burnet, is a sign that the society has come of age.

Behind these changes stands that transformation that would

be so fascinating to explore if we had time, the transformation of the Australian people into a highly industrialised and still more urban society, presenting such unexpected complexity and demanding the whole spectrum of modern skills. This expanding society and its exposure to an uneasy world will require all the toughness and elasticity of mind the Australian can summon up. I have to say in concluding these lectures that I have no fear that he will fail.

Australian critics may not seem to share this confidence. "The individual Australian," writes Professor Partridge, "has acquired, whether justly or not, a reputation for fearlessness, forthrightness and independence. On the whole, these qualities have not yet been remarkably conspicuous in the nation's intellectual or cultural life: the fundamental ideas which inform its art, literature, political, social and moral thought, are almost always ideas which have originated elsewhere. It is doubtful whether in this period the Australian community has succeeded in becoming a notably reflective, critical or fertile one." [11] But Professor Partridge himself recognizes that it is early to judge: in a country which only in the last ten or twenty years has moved into that scale of intellectual activity which enables a more than spasmodic originality, it is more useful to look at its type of mind than at its mental achievement. Let the works of genius wait: they will come, in their own time, and when and where we least expect them. Meanwhile, Professor Partridge's comment is itself typical of the habits of mind of many contemporary Australian intellectuals who turn a sceptical and critical eye on any too-ready sign of self-satisfaction. It is in keeping that contemporary Australian poetry has been strong in self-satire, notably in A. D. Hope's "Dunciad Minimus" and in James McAuley's "True Discovery of Australia." [12] It will

11. In Greenwood, *Australia*, p. 414.
12. The "Dunciad Minimus" remains unpublished except for extracts. McAuley's poem appears in his *Under Aldebaran* (Melbourne University Press, 1946).

be remembered that Swift placed Lilliput "north-west of Van Diemen's Land, in latitude 30°S (approximately the position of Lake Torrens)" in South Australia; and McAuley takes Gulliver as "our True Discoverer"—"Who found his Lilliput where you will find Lilliput still, and more so than before."

Let Gulliver report:

XIII

The place, my lord, is much like Gideon's fleece
The second time he laid it on the ground;
For by the will of God it has remained
Bone-dry itself, with water all around.

XIV

Yet, as a wheel that's driven in the ruts
It has a wet rim where the people clot
Like mud; and though they praise the inner spaces,
When asked to go themselves, they'd rather not.

XV

The men are brave, contentious, ignorant;
The women very much as one expects.
For their religion, I must be excused,
Having no stomach to observe their sects.

XVI

You must be wary in your conversation;
For, seeing them thumb-high, you might suppose
They recognized your stature, but beware!
Their notion of themselves is grandiose.

XVII

And you will often find, although their heads
Are like a berry on a twig of bones,
They speak as Giants of the South Pacific
And treat the islands as their stepping-stones.

XVIII

North-east across the water, Brobdingnag
Casts its momentous shadow on the sea
And fills the sky with thunder: but they smile
And sit on their verandahs taking tea,

XIX

Watching through the pleasant afternoons
Flood fire and cyclone in successive motion
Complete the work the pioneers began
Of shifting all the soil into the ocean.

.   .   .   .

XXVI

Mentally, they're still in Pliocene,
A flat terrain impermeably dense;
And will be so, until volcanic mind
Arches its back at brute indifference.

And McAuley adds his

   —private Envoi or reflective Coda
   To readers fit though few: in a country where
   An acorn-cup would seem a scotch-and-soda,

XXXVIII

A man of even middling parts will look
So tall, he may forget his real status,
And play the sorry fable of the frog
Who burst his belly with his own afflatus.

The savour is astringent, and not to all palates; and yet on the whole we find ourselves at ease with it. Stephen Toulmin, the Oxford philosopher now at Leeds, who was with us in Melbourne for a year, wrote in a recent Manchester Guardian review: "At the heart of their view of themselves and of all else lies an impatience ... with exaggeration, with pretentiousness. ... This attitude can be destructive of idealism and aspirations, but it could turn into a mature and adult scepticism, consistent with the kind of political and intellectual stamina one meets among the best Australian scholars." [13]

Of course, astringent satire is not the daily fare even of the tougher Australian thinkers; but it merely exaggerates a quality that is common among the best of our younger scholars. It is

13. Review of J. D. Pringle, *Australian Accent* (London, 1958), in *The Manchester Guardian Weekly*, 9 October 1958.

true that the lessons which one generation has learned, the next may forget; but one knows, looking in at one's own experience and out at that of others, that we have shared a passage from generous but relatively naive beliefs through the disillusioning experience of our middle years to a more sober understanding; and one sees the best of our pupils of a younger generation grasping the end-point of our common pilgrimage as we present it to them, with less need of wasteful journeying. For the mediocre, it is true, this can result in deflating dullness; but in the better minds it shows itself as an honest clarity of vision, an intellectual habit of sticking close to the contours of the question asked, of demanding to see it clear. In politics, it makes for a distrust of the doctrinaire that fits an old Australian tradition, only temporarily disturbed by the aberrations of this century. In intellectual enquiry, it is not antipathetic to the abstract question, but it is impatient of vagueness. In literature, it might seem destructive of that strong vein of idealism which I stressed in my second lecture. But, indeed, satire is the weapon of the idealist once bitten but twice shy. Scratch him but lightly, and you will find his expectation of wonder showing through. He builds his cities like other cities, but still expects the blossoming of his museum land to be unlike any other, hoping, as one of our more satirical poets wrote, but scarcely in satire—

> hoping, if still from deserts the prophets come,
> Such savage and scarlet as no green hills dare
> Springs in that waste. . . .[14]

It was of an earlier generation that Arthur Adams wrote in "The Australian":

> So, toward undreamt-of destinies
> He slouches down the centuries.[15]

14. A. D. Hope, "Australia," in George Mackaness, ed., *An Anthology of Australian Verse* (Sydney: Angus and Robertson, 1952).
15. In Mackaness, *An Anthology of Australian Verse.*

And that is true too: the easy slouch, the astringent irony, the direct look, and behind these things, the awaiting and unlimited expectation, all these are true of him, and leaven the mediocrity that is in his as in any other community. And after all it is the "Terra Australis" of James McAuley, whose Lilliputian satire I have already quoted, which best states these things (and perhaps I should explain that the angophora is a tree of fantastic gestures and that the call of the white cockatoo is as he describes it). I quote the two middle verses of the four which make the poem:

It is your land of similes: the wattle
Scatters its pollen on the doubting heart;
The flowers are wide-awake; the air gives ease.
There you come home; the magpies call you Jack
And whistle like larrikins at you from the trees.

There too the angophora preaches on the hillsides
With the gestures of Moses; and the white cockatoo
Perched on his limbs, screams with demoniac pain;
And who shall say on what errand the insolent emu
Walks between morning and night on the edge of the plain? [16]

16. In *Under Aldebaran.*

Index